Mom, The tit... [barcode] P9-CJX-744 Anne

Everyone Loves Erma!

Xmas 2001

(For more cheers, please turn page)

By Erma Bombeck:

AT WIT'S END*
"JUST WAIT TILL YOU HAVE CHILDREN OF
    YOUR OWN!" (with Bil Keane)*
IF LIFE IS A BOWL OF CHERRIES—WHAT AM I
    DOING IN THE PITS?*
I LOST EVERYTHING IN THE POST-NATAL DEPRESSION*
AUNT ERMA'S COPE BOOK: How to Get From
    Monday to Friday…in 12 Days*
MOTHERHOOD: The Second Oldest Profession
THE GRASS IS ALWAYS GREENER OVER THE
    SEPTIC TANK*
FAMILY: The Ties That Bind…and Gag!*
I WANT TO GROW UP, I WANT TO GROW HAIR, I
    WANT TO GO TO BOISE

*Published by Fawcett Books

FAMILY

The Ties That Bind . . . And Gag!

Erma Bombeck

FAWCETT CREST • NEW YORK

A Fawcett Crest Book
Published by The Ballantine Publishing Group
Copyright © 1987 by Erma Bombeck

All rights reserved under International and Pan-American Copyright Conventions. Published in the United States by The Ballantine Publishing Group, a division of Random House, Inc., New York, and simultaneously in Canada by Random House of Canada Limited, Toronto. Some material in this book is based on material that has appeared elsewhere in another form.

Fawcett Crest and colophon are trademarks of Random House, Inc.

Some material in this book is based on material that has appeared elsewhere in another form.

www.randomhouse.com/BB/

Library of Congress Catalog Card Number: 87-3277

ISBN 0-449-21529-6

This edition published by arrangement with McGraw-Hill Book Company, a division of McGraw-Hill, Inc.

Printed in Canada

First Ballantine Books Edition: December 1988

30 29 28 27 26 25 24 23

TO BILL BOMBECK:
WHO HAD DEFINITE IDEAS
OF THE CONCEPTION OF THESE CHARACTERS
LONG BEFORE I HAD IDEAS OF PUTTING
THEM INTO A BOOK.

CONTENTS

Contents

FAMILY

The Ties That Bind . . . And Gag!

THE FAMILY: 1936

It was the best of times.

I had my own watch, a tricycle, and a clip-on Shirley Temple hair ribbon that covered the entire right side of my head. My mother wore an apron and silk stockings and baked every day. She looked like Betty Crocker looked before her face-lift, pierced ears and junk to make her hair fat.

The family . . . all four of us . . . sat on the front porch in the summer and talked about the squeak in the swing. My dad always told me to get my tricycle off the sidewalk at night before someone fell over it. I never did. My mother cleaned the living room every day. We never sat in it. Once I turned on one of the lights and the cellophane around the lamp shade smelled and I got my hands slapped.

Mom cut the grass and filled the clothesline every day. Every Friday, she hosed out the garbage cans. In the spring she really got crazy . . . lugging mattresses out to the backyard and setting up curtain rods to dry the lace curtains. Sometimes, she put on gloves and hat with her best dress and took the streetcar into town where she went from store to store paying the utilities and making fifty-cent payments on my watch and tricycle.

My sister bossed and went to high school. She didn't do anything else. I was insanely busy going to school and being a servant to everyone . . . running to the store ten thousand times a day for my mother, and whenever the pan under the icebox filled with water from the melting ice, you-know-who always had to empty it without spilling a single drop.

One morning my father didn't get up and go to work. He went to the hospital and died the next day.

I hadn't thought that much about him before. He was just someone who left and came home and seemed glad to see everyone at night. He opened the jar of pickles when no one else could. He was the only one in the house who wasn't afraid to go into the basement by himself.

He cut himself shaving, but no one kissed it or got excited about it. It was understood when it rained, he got the car and brought it around to the door. When anyone was sick, he went out to get the prescription filled. He took lots of pictures . . . but he was never in them.

Whenever I played house, the mother doll had a lot to do. I never knew what to do with the daddy doll, so I had him say, "I'm going off to work now" and threw him under the bed.

The funeral was in our living room and a lot of people came and brought all kinds of good food and cakes. We had never had so much company before.

I went to my room and felt under the bed for the daddy doll. When I found him, I dusted him off and put him on my bed.

He never did anything. I didn't know his leaving would hurt so much.

The creditors came the day after the funeral and carted off the icebox, the car, and the contents of the living room that no one ever sat in.

Grandma came and said she was taking us all home with her so we could be a "family" again. The family got bigger and a lot weirder. There were Mother's sister and her husband and their two children, a brother who played pool all day, and another sister who roller-skated and was about to be married. There was also my grandfather, who never made a left-hand turn and who used lard to polish the car.

Grandma wore an apron and was always busy cleaning the living room that no one ever sat in. The kitchen was the only room in the house that had heat and that was when the oven was lit. I used to stand on the chair to get warm and look down on everyone as they argued about money.

My mother got a job. No one in my entire class had a mother who went to work every morning. I didn't tell anyone but my best friend. She got mad at me and spread it all over school.

In 1938, my mother said, "We are going to be a family again" (again!) and introduced us to a stepfather. I was the only girl in North America to have a stepfather. I didn't take a chance on telling even my best friend.

My stepfather and I didn't talk to one another for awhile. I guess he was a person who didn't know how to show love. I remember when he taught me how to ride a two-wheel bicycle. I told him not to let go, but he said it was time. I fell and Mom ran to pick me up, but he waved her off. I was so mad I showed him. I got right back on that bike and rode it myself. He didn't even feel embarrassed. He just smiled.

When I went to college, he didn't hang around to talk like Mom did . . . he just lugged fifteen pieces of luggage up to the third floor and acted sorta awkward.

Whenever I called home, he acted like he wanted to talk, but he always said, "I'll get your mother."

All my life he nagged, "Where are you going? What time are you coming home? Do you have gas in the car? Who's going to be there? No, you can't go."

It was a long time before I realized that's how you love someone.

My mother selfishly pursued a career on a factory assembly line making rubber door strips for General Motors cars. My stepfather dedicated his life to making me pick up towels in the bathroom and turning off lights.

I could hardly wait to get married, leave home, and have a "family" of my own with a living room that no one ever sat in.

THE FAMILY: 1987

Friday: 5 P.M.

For no reason I was like a nervous hostess, re-arranging the drapery folds, pushing chairs under the table, and sliding down the coffee table on the seat of my pants to transfer the dust to a place where few people ever looked anymore.

In a few minutes the tranquility would give way to three grown children coming home for the weekend to pose for the traditional Christmas card picture.

"Are they here yet?" yelled my husband, balancing his tripod and camera.

I shook my head and walked quickly to the living room where I flipped on the light. It was as I remembered it. The white sofas facing one another, the pristine plush carpet, and the plump pillows that peaked like fresh meringue.

"What do I smell?" he asked, slipping off his shoes before he entered the room.

"Cellophane from the lamp shades. I wonder what's keeping them."

"Them" are two sons and one daughter, conceived in passion, carried with heartburn, and raised with love. We share the same genes, chromosomes, and last name. We have never eaten the same breakfast cereal, watched the same TV shows, liked the same people, or spoken the same language.

Why wouldn't they be late? In thirty years, not once have our bodies been on the same time cycle.

When I was on wash, iron, shop, cook, and run . . . they were on perma-sleep and off. When I was on sleep and exhaustion, they were on spin-around-the-crib, damp-dry, and fill. Even as they got older, when I went to bed, they were going out. When I got up for breakfast, they were coming in.

"How did you get all of them to come in the first place? You know how they hate to sit for these things."

"I told them we were reading the will."

I wondered why we bothered at all. Last year's picture had one kid sitting on the sofa in a tie and sport coat. He was not wearing shoes. Our daughter was looking straight into the camera with her eyes closed, and another son was hanging over my shoulder with a temperature of 102. The dog was

7

licking himself in a disgusting area. All of our eyes (with the exception of our daughter and the dog) were focused on a blurred hand and knee coming into the frame which belonged to my husband. It wasn't a picture you'd want to see on a religious holiday.

Why couldn't we be like our old neighbors, the Nelsons? Every year we got a card from them with their entire family gathered in front of the fireplace in their ski sweaters and capped-teeth smiles.

"Did you talk with our son in L.A.?"

"I left a message on his machine," I said.

Actually, I had not talked with my son in person for over three years. I talked to his answering machine, he talked to my answering machine, and sometimes our answering machines talked to one another. I wouldn't admit this to many people, but his machine and I had a better relationship than we did. His machine had such fine manners. I'd call and it would say softly, "Hi, I'm not here right now but if you would leave your name and your phone number, I'll get back to you as soon as I can. At the sound of the beep, you have ten seconds. Have a good day now."

My son would never have said that.

The machine was so nice, I could never bring myself to say what I had planned to say. "You bum! I have stretch marks around my knees and you don't have five minutes to call your mother." So I'd end up by saying, "I know you're busy, dear. I was just checking to see if you're alive. I hardly hurt at all today. You have a good day too.''

It would be nice to have the family together again, sitting around rekindling memories, catching up on their lives, seeing the legacy we created . . . the monument, so to speak, to our own immortality. My reverie was broken by the sound of car doors. Our older son kicked open the door. ''Anyone home?'' (I hated it when he looked me in the eye and said that!)

He was wearing a wrinkled jacket with sleeves pushed up to the elbow, Hawaiian shirt, and balloon pants that revealed white ankles and bare feet.

His father turned to me and said, ''For God's sake, Erma, didn't you tell your son we were going to take the family picture for our Christmas card?''

''That's why I'm here,'' he said.

''So, why didn't you shave?''

''I did, just a few hours ago.''

''Did you put a blade in?''

''Sure, it's the new stubble look like *Miami Vice*. Don't tell me you haven't seen it before.''

''Of course I've seen it before . . . on winos and travelers whose luggage has been lost for three weeks.''

''Dad, it's sexy. Gives you that I-just-rolled-out-of-the-sack look. You remember that. Hey, Mom, I'm going over to the coast for a couple of days to catch some rays. How about baby-sitting my pet.''

''I don't need another dog. Is it messy?''

"Mom, would I leave you with anything messy? It's all here . . . food and all. No sweat, honest."

"You know how the neighbors feel about barking dogs."

"I promise you. This animal won't bark. I'll put him in the utility room. His food is in by the toaster."

At that moment, his brother kicked open the front door. "I hope you're satisfied," he announced flatly. "I have a cold."

My eyes misted and I grabbed his arm. "It's wonderful having you here. How long can you stay?"

"It depends on how long it takes to do this much laundry," he said, thrusting his suitcase at me. "Everything I own is dirty."

We said hello to our daughter.

She returned the greeting with, "My transmission sounds funny."

The moment had come. My husband began arranging and draping their bodies over the sofa before he looked into the lens.

"What does it look like?" I asked.

"It looks like a group of illegal aliens hauled in for questioning. What are you doing in a tennis dress?" he asked our daughter.

"Playing tennis," she said dryly. "I didn't know it was formal."

"This is a Christmas card, for crying out loud. Go get into something appropriate. Come on, boys! Stand up straight!"

"I am," said our son. "I just don't have shoes on."

"Then stand behind your mother. No, that won't work. The nuclear mushroom on your T-shirt is hovering just above your mother's head. My God! What is he doing in an antinuclear T-shirt anyway?"

"It was the only thing left in my closet that was clean."

"So go get one of my shirts. Now where's your sister?"

"She's washing her hair."

"Is this going to take long?"

"His feet smell."

"Where's the dog? We can't have a picture without Harry in it."

"Quit shoving."

"Creep!"

The family. We were a strange little band of characters trudging through life sharing diseases and toothpaste, coveting one another's desserts, hiding shampoo, borrowing money, locking each other out of our rooms, inflicting pain and kissing to heal it in the same instant, loving, laughing, defending, and trying to figure out the common thread that bound us all together.

Sitting there I thought about how the years have challenged families in a way no one would have thought it possible to survive. They've weathered combinations of step, foster, single, adoptive, surrogate, frozen embryo, and sperm bank. They've multiplied, divided, extended, and banded into communes. They've been assaulted by technology, battered by sexual revolutions, and confused by role reversals. But they're still here—playing to a full house.

One by one the family wandered into frame with wet hair, borrowed shirt, and shoes that didn't fit.

As I struggled to give dignity to the moment, my daughter said, "Mom, why do you have a snake in your utility room?"

The camera clicked. The annual Christmas card portrait was captured for another year. One son sat there in the same sport coat and tie he had worn last year and the same bare feet. The other one's mouth was crooked as he whispered out of the side of it how he felt like throwing up since the plane was late and he hadn't eaten. The dog was licking the same disgusting part he had licked the year before. Our daughter's eyes were following the blurred figure of her father trying to find his place before the shutter clicked. My lips were forming what looked like the SH word . . . when in fact it was the SN word. They photograph the same.

Immediately following the picture-taking, the shoving began and didn't stop until a body hit the floor. Another one felt compelled to tell me her brother had gotten into the dip because she smelled the cream cheese on his breath. Echoes of "I'm telling" resounded. The stories began to flow . . .

about the time they locked the baby sitter out in the snow, the day the aquarium caught fire in their bedroom, the school play where one was a dangling participle, and who spit on plates when it was his turn to do the dishes.

They had all returned from their private lives, but the moment we were together, the floodgates of the past opened and once again we slipped into the comfortable role of a family.

One by one, stories were resurrected of the fun times we had shared. We must have sat there for five or ten minutes.

"TRUST ME . . .
I'M YOUR MOTHER"

Friday: 6:30 P.M.

Mother backed into the kitchen from the garage balancing her handbag, a shopping bag, and a large hatbox. "Something smells good," she said, kicking the door shut with her foot.

"Onion tops in the disposer," I said. "You didn't have to bring dessert."

"I know. Put it on a plate and I'll take my box back, thank you."

She lifted off the lid, "Doesn't that smell good?"

"It smells like fruitcake and I hate fruitcake."

"I don't understand you," she said. "Your grandfather loved fruitcake."

"What has that got to do with me?"

14

"He loved you so. You were his favorite. The pineapple alone cost $6."

"I hate pineapple, Mother."

"It's Julia Child's recipe and you like Julia Child."

The conversation was inane and predictable. Why didn't I just admit that people who love fruitcake are . . . "different." In evangelism, they are to the right of Jerry Falwell and Pat Robertson. In fact, I wouldn't be surprised if fruitcake lovers founded the next major religion of the twentieth century.

I have never met a fruitcake baker in my life who didn't want to convert me to all that baked fruit. I could be standing in Mother's kitchen and announce without a trace of humor, "I do not like fruitcake. I have never liked fruitcake. I have sampled more than 10,000 species of fruitcake, and it is my dream that I never have to sample it again," only to have her put a slice before me and say, "Try it. This one is different."

Fruitcakes are not different. They all tend to be the same, each having an assortment of incompatible fruits and the distinction of weighing more than the stove they were cooked in. They defy all of the culinary rules in the book. No one ever says, "This fruitcake is so light, you don't know you're eating it." That is because the heavier the fruitcake . . . the better.

Another thing I hate about fruitcake lovers is they smile when their cake is rejected. I don't like people who do that. It's unnatural. I'd be more comfortable if they would just say, "Who asked you to eat this cake? It cost me $45 to make, and if it were up to me, I'd drop it on your ungrateful foot!" You can have respect for a person like that. But no, fruitcake lovers will stand by and watch you spit out the sample in your hand and say, "But isn't it moist?"

"You are so stubborn," said Mother, transferring the industrial-strength cake to a plate. "My son-in-law will like it."

Now that had been one of the greatest surprises of my married life. The man at the wedding who was "not good enough" to marry me has now turned out to be worth two of me. I never thought she'd turn on me. Mothers are supposed to be loyal to their own kids . . . right or wrong. It just didn't work out that way. My husband would bring her a bouquet of fresh flowers for some occasion and she'd say, "Erma never got me flowers that you don't have to dust." Or when we'd climb into a car she'd say, "I never got to ride in the front seat before. Erma always said if I rolled down the windows, I wouldn't get sick back there."

After the children came, she really put her longevity in the family to the test. I was pitching out uneaten food from the kids' plates one night when my husband said, "Aren't you going to save any of that?"

I looked to Mother for support. She looked at me like I was something that had just missed the trap set under the sink for me and said, "Waste not, want not. Lord knows that's not how she was raised. We never could get her to see the value of money. Maybe if she were out there like you, earning it, she'd be more frugal.''

Throughout the years, my husband has been treated to the history of my stubbornness, my dedication to spending more money than I have, my bad temper, lack of patience, inability to finish anything, short interest span, and refusal to set goals.

I often thought of going home to Mother, but what for? My husband would be there . . . eating fruitcake!

"So, are you all set for Thanksgiving at your place?" I asked. "I told the kids and they're looking forward to it."

"Sure . . . unless you'd like to have dinner here?"

"Mom," I said, "you know you enjoy all that fussing around surrounded by family . . . trotting out your best dishes and all that last-minute excitement. Besides, no one can turn out a picture-book turkey like you do. I don't know how you do it year after year." Mom smiled and was caught up in her own thoughts.

Erma pulls that "Grandma enjoys it" line on me every year! What enjoyment! What makes all of them think a sixty-five-year-old woman likes to get up at 4 A.M., arm-wrestle a naked turkey, stand over a toaster trying to make stale bread into fresh dressing, and spend ten hours making a meal that will take twelve minutes to inhale? Easy for her. All she brings is a bag of nacho chips and four folding chairs.

As for the picture-book turkey, the only thing I share with that animal is a thigh problem! Everyone thinks turkeys are fun-loving gobble-gobbles. If they cooked one, they'd see them as the vindictive, grudge-wielding, give-it-to-them-with-your-last-breath, revenge-seeking, tough old birds they are.

No one understands that a turkey gets done . . . any time it feels like it. I've had 30-pound birds cook in two hours: before the pies have cooled, before the potatoes and yams have cooked, before the cranberries are frozen . . . before the guests have left home.

And I've seen 10-pound turkeys cook for eight hours and still look like you're carving a ham.

Makes you wonder if the first Thanksgiving in Massachusetts was the religious experience the history books say it was.

Wouldn't be surprised if Mrs. Brewster really sent the kids out in the morning for an egg corn McMeal breakfast and told them if they set foot in her kitchen before the turkey was done she'd kill 'em.

The pictures of the first Thanksgiving always look so idyllic with Indians embracing white men in a show of peace and harmony. I can't believe there wasn't a disgruntled hostess somewhere who said, "If Running Deer wants to smoke that stinking pipe, he's going to have to go outside and do it."

She used to pull the same scam at Christmas

with the toys until I pulled her cork. "Why don't you leave the drum set at Grandma's," she'd say, "so you'll have something to play with when you visit." Those drums sounded like a thousand camels on your eyelids.

"I've invited your cousin Marie and her husband for Thanksgiving," said Mom. "These dish towels could use a shot of bleach."

"I thought you weren't speaking to her because her daughter never thanked you for the pen and pencil set you sent her for graduation."

"She finally sent a note," she said. "Besides, I don't like to hold grudges."

Right. And if you believed that, you'd believe that every Friday night Nancy Reagan watches *Falcon Crest*. My mother has elevated revenge to an art form.

Every year at the family reunion, we all check in with her to see whom we are speaking to and who is out in the cold. The length of their sentence varies with their crimes.

"You didn't answer your phone when I called because you knew it was me." (four years)

"You never paid me back the $3 I put in for you when we went in on flowers for Margaret's funeral." (eighteen years)

"I was the last to hear you were expecting." (two years)

"When you looked through my photo albums,

my picture of Dad was there. When you left, it was gone." (twenty-five years)

"YOU know!" (This was the dreaded grudge that lasted for life.)

I remember going to one reunion where you needed a program to know which side of the picnic table to sit on. I approached my cousin Doris and said, "Are we speaking to one another this year?"

"I don't think so," she said.

"Why?"

"I never sent your mother an invitation to Robbie's birthday party."

"How old is Robbie now?"

"Thirty-six."

I picked up my plate to move. "What about Estelle? Am I speaking to her?"

"Not unless she returned the bread pan that your mother sent home with her twenty years ago."

"It will be good to see Marie again," I said to Mother. "I haven't seen her since the reunion when she grabbed the last picnic table in the shade."

Mother's head shot up. "Was that Marie?"

"Forget it. I was probably mistaken," I said quickly. "So, how are you two lovebirds enjoying Dad's retirement?"

"Wonderful," she said. "Yesterday your father cleaned out the exhaust fan and tomorrow he's going to take the lime out of the teakettle."

"What did he do today?"

"Showed me how to walk with my legs spread

apart so I wouldn't wear a path down the middle of the hallway carpet.''

''And to think we were worried about you two getting on one another's nerves.''

If my daughter had sense, she'd worry. I could write the book on nerves. Maybe a primer and coloring book for wives of retired husbands everywhere.

See Jim.

Jim used to run and jump and chase clients. Jim stays home now. He has a new watch. He will tell you what time it is even if you don't want to know.

It is time to get up.

It is time to remove the oil stain from the driveway before it spreads to the rest of the house.

It is time to alphabetize your spices.

It is time to eat (lunch/dinner/breakfast/break/snack/party).

Sometimes Jim will act like a houseguest.

''Where do you hide the iced tea glasses?''

''The hall bath needs toilet tissue, Mother.''

''There is someone at the door selling something.''

''I'd put the dishes away, but I don't know where they belong.''

Sometimes Jim will act like he has hired you for the summer.

''Who was that on the phone and what did they want?''

"Where are you going and what time are you coming back?"

"I don't think that grass can wait another day."

Retired men like Jim bring efficiency to the home. It is cheaper to make your own tea bags than to buy them ready-made.

Don't heat up the oven for one baked potato. Do a dozen at a time and freeze them.

See Jim drive a nail by the door to hold your car keys.

See him drive a nail by the phone to hold a pencil.

See Jim drive a nail in the desk to hold your unpaid bills.

See Jim drive you crazy.

It was all a surprise. I didn't know I married a man who knew so much about dishwashers, wax build-up, hand-washables, stain removers, children, and how to keep bananas from turning brown.

Jim is surprised. He does not know how I have managed to stumble through forty-five years of running a house without him.

Everyone is surprised he is busier than ever.

I'm not.

As I filled a glass of water at the sink and popped an aspirin in my mouth, Mom said, "Don't you feel good?"

"Just a little headache," I said.

"Nonsense," she said. "You probably need a laxative."

"YOU'RE NOT SICK . . . YOU'RE IRREGULAR"

Scientific breakthroughs have come and gone in this country and have been ignored totally by my mother. No one will ever convince her that the responsibility for good health does not lie within the minds of each and every one of us.

From birth, my mother's cure-all for every malady I ever suffered was the same, "You need a laxative." I went through grade school wondering why children went around with their legs and arms in a cast when all they had to do to get well was to take a candy-flavored cleansing agent before they went to bed.

It was uncanny how she could just look at you and determine how you were ready for a clean start in life. A laxative cured an upset stomach, headache, fever, stomach rashes, dizziness, and general run-down feeling. By the time she finished with you, nothing seemed important enough to open your mouth and complain about.

Around the age of twelve, she varied her diagnosis to include, "You're just bored." All my friends had impacted teeth, blood disorders, viral attacks, appendicitis, dog bites, and pneumonia. I had all those things, but I was "just bored" and the cure was, "Get yourself something to do or I'll find something."

After I was married, she offered still another second opinion: "It's just your nerves."

"Mom, I fainted twice today." ("It's just your nerves.")

"I think I'm pregnant." ("Nonsense, it's just your nerves.")

She stuck to her story even after I gave birth to an 8-pound, 4-ounce bundle of nerves.

No one in this family has ever taken my illnesses seriously. Just once I'd like to get a virus that everyone else in town doesn't have. I seem to be the last adult female in North America to get it. I don't ask for Mother Teresa, but I deserve a little compassion, especially from my husband.

"I don't feel well," I said to him one morning. "I feel like my chest has been wound too tight. Pain is tap-dancing across my eyes. I save up my coughs until I feel adventurous."

"Nonsense," said my husband, "you're just bored. Everyone in the office has what you have.

There's a lot of it going around and the diagnosis is they probably just need a career change.''

"You could be right," I said. "I don't want to be married anymore."

"Sometimes," he continued, "it's just an attitude where you tell yourself you're sick, when in reality you are generally discontented with yourself. I've seen a million cases of this at work."

"You didn't say that when you went to bed for three days after you had your teeth cleaned."

"That's different," he said. "I had complications."

"A popcorn hull embedded in a molar?"

I think my trouble is I cannot communicate what I feel to my doctor. As for him, I have yet to understand one word of what he is saying. He speaks Latin . . . I speak *Reader's Digest.*

Most people are like that. Ever since I told a crowd in a doctor's waiting room that I had a Bavarian cyst and two others had the same thing, I've been convinced we do not speak the same language. I suspect I am intimidated by anyone who wears white all winter and washes his hands 137 times a day. God, I'm insecure.

"You say I have this problem in my humorous bone? As in Woody Allen?"

"Not that humerus."

"Would you spell that please?"

"Of course," he says. "Give me a piece of scrap paper and I'll make a diagram and label it for you."

''Here, just tear off part of the gown you gave me.''

There is nothing more humiliating in this world than to try to explain to your husband what the doctor said. ''It has something to do with my nose,'' I say.

''What part of your nose?''

''You know. The rect . . . ''

''Try septum,'' he says. ''What's wrong with it?''

''It's perverted.''

''Deviated.''

''Same thing.''

I've talked with people who told me that they had a cather inserted in them for a week (not to be confused with Willa).

Another friend I know could never remember his blood pressure numbers but said if his diabolic reading was under his golf score, he was happy.

When my grandmother once announced that she had a prostate deficiency and was told it wasn't possible, she snapped, ''The way I eat, anything is possible.''

As one of the kids joined Mother and me at the table, I sneezed and blew my nose. ''Are you coming down with something?'' he asked.

''She's just bored,'' said my mother. ''Here, why don't you take a shot of this cough syrup.''

''I'm not well enough to take that,'' I said.

''What do you mean you're not well enough?'' she said.

"Read!"

In bold letters the label warned if you exceeded the recommended dosage you could suffer from nervousness, dizziness, and sleeplessness. You could not take the medicine at all if you suffered from high blood pressure, heart disease, diabetes, or thyroid disease, or were presently taking a prescription antihypertensive or antidepressant drug containing a monoamine oxidase inhibitor. It was not to be taken if you had glaucoma, asthma, or difficulty in urination due to enlargement of the prostate gland.

"You could chance it," said my son, "and if you get a reaction contact the Poison Control Center as soon as possible."

"Here's one you can possibly take," said Mother, grabbing another bottle. "Let's see. Are you pregnant or a nursing mother?" (I groaned.) "Just checking. Do you have an ulcer? Are you allergic to aspirin or do you have a bleeding disease?"

"What's a bleeding disease?"

"You'd blame me," she said, tossing it back.

"How about this one?" asked my son. "The side effects are dryness of mouth, drowsiness, temporary blurred vision, dilation of the pupils, disorientation, memory disturbances, dizziness, restlessness, hallucinations, confusion, skin irritation, dry, itchy, red eyes, and you can't operate any dangerous machinery."

"Unless that includes the stove, forget it," I said.

"Put these on the top shelf," I said.

"Why?" asked my son. "There are no children here."

"These should be kept out of the reach of sick people."

"I hope you're not going to ruin the holidays for everyone," said my mother.

"Grandma, you sound just like Mom when we were little. Every time someone asked Mom what we were getting for Christmas, she said, 'I really don't know. Either a chest cold, stomach flu, or walking diarrhea. They always come up with something . . . even if it is at the last minute.' "

It was true. I don't know if it was the anticipation and excitement of the season or the wear and tear of the end of the year, but the kids fell apart on schedule every holiday.

We always used to hear stories of Christmas . . . about how people went to parties or watched the big tree at the courthouse being lit up. Once when I was at the drugstore having prescriptions filled, I even saw a group of people singing. I didn't know what it was all about so I asked the druggist. He said, "They're called carolers and they go out and sing in front of homes and sometimes they're invited in for punch and cookies."

"But how do they get their medication?" I asked.

"They're not sick," he said.

Not sick! That was the first time I realized that not everyone got sick at Christmas. It made me curious about how other people spent the holidays. All I know is in our neighborhood of cookie-cutter houses in the suburbs, flushed faces and fevers were a way of life.

We'd fix a buffet of antibiotics, clear broth, 7-Up, and Jell-O, hoist a glass of Kaopectate, and propose our traditional toast, "TO MENOPAUSE."

"MOM, WE'LL TAKE
CARE OF HIM"

As Grandma made her exit, I collared my son and said, "About the snake."

"Mom," he said, "there is no need to hyperventilate. It's just for a couple of days. Besides, I thought mothers were supposed to be there for their children."

"You show me a boy who brings a snake home to his mother and I'll show you an orphan."

His siblings joined us. "She was the same way when we wanted to bring Harry into the house, remember? 'Don't feed him at the table. Go wash your hands. Don't kiss that dog, you don't know where he's been.' "

"Now he follows you around all day," said my son.

"You'd be lost without him," said my daughter wistfully.

"Sometimes I think you love that dog more than you love us, admit it."

Admit what! Harry is a bundle of bad breath who should be owned by an attorney. He never passes a thigh without sinking his teeth into it. He bites the hand that feeds him. Mine. And there were promises made the day he came into the house that were never kept.

He would never be fed from the table. (True, he had his own chair alongside the rest of the family.) He would sleep in his own bed (providing it was a waterbed filled with Perrier). Whenever he piddled or dropped a bomb in the house, it would be cleaned up by the first person who saw it. (Astigmatisms flourished.) He would be trained by the children to do his business outside. (He has lived with paper so long, we bought him a subscription to the *New York Times*.)

Today he is eight years old, and if you can visualize a fifty-six-year-old man in a shaggy fur coat who watches television for six hours each evening and never leaves the room for a commercial, you got it.

Harry knows nothing about nature. He has never seen a tree, a blade of grass, a curb, a pillar, or a car tire.

He has no curiosity as to why the velvet on the chair is so hard for him to relieve himself on, or why they would make a plush carpet so difficult to balance yourself on three legs.

31

Heaven knows I tried. I praised him when he went where he was supposed to, and I punished him when he missed the paper. It always worked for the kids.

When the house became carpeted with wall-to-wall urine and our guests had to keep moving lest they be mistaken for a wall, we installed a doggy door.

The doggy door is an 8½-by-12½-inch opening cut into a $400 door. To the dog, it is like jumping the Snake River . . . blindfolded . . . on a tractor mower.

The training proved to be rather simple. Within an hour, I figured out if you pushed the plastic insert with your nose hard enough, it opened to the outside, and it was just a matter of trying to jump for a little impetus, balancing your paws on the sill, and pushing yourself through.

It took Harry a little longer to comprehend.

"Do not look upon it as the Berlin Wall," I said one day as I rubbed my raw shoulder. "It's a two-way street. You can go out and you can come back in whenever you please."

One of the kids came in one day full of excitement. "Mom, Harry is standing at the door trying to get out!"

Unfortunately, it was not the door we put the hole in.

One day I was in the kitchen when I heard a dog authority on a talk show. The host was asking him what to do when a dog wet on the same chair all the time. I dropped the dish towel and ran in just in time to hear the dog authority smile and say, "Throw away the chair!"

When a dog allows you to become his best friend, you owe him . . . big. Food is his primary source of pleasure.

My husband came into the kitchen one night, dipped his spoon into a bowl, and said "Ummm. Tastes terrific. What is it?"

I said, "Chicken, bacon bits, onions, and kidneys."

"What do you call it?"

"I call it the dog's dinner. We're having beans and franks. Go get washed up."

"Do I want to know what's in this bottle filled with brown fluid?"

"It's a new beverage for dogs who are 'sick of drinking just water.' It's flavored with beef."

"That's quite a jump for someone who drinks from a toilet," he said. "Besides, how do you know our dog is sick of drinking just water? Does he say yuck and spit it out?"

My husband had a point. We've never had a dog who sang, talked, wrote notes, or communicated with us in any way.

"We just have to trust someone," I said.

And trust we have. During the last few years I've seen the selection of dog food grow from a couple of bags of nuggets by the grass seed near the door to an entire aisle of options. On blind faith, I've lugged in cheese and beef pellets, dry food that turns sensuous in its own gravy, jerky snacks, liver-flavored cookies, bones that whiten dogs' teeth, and cans of gourmet dog food to combat boredom.

"Let me ask you a question," said my husband. "Has this dog ever gotten excited about any dog products touted on TV?"

"You know the only time he reacts to anything on TV is when he goes to bed during PBS pledge week."

"He doesn't care," said my husband. "For all we know, he's probably a vegetarian and doesn't know how to tell us. We could throw him a raw potato every day and he'd be happy as a clam." He tilted the bottle of beef-flavored drink, took a sip, and winced.

"What did you expect, gusto?"

He looked at the dog and whispered, "Stick to the toilet."

Despite all the demands pets put on you, in the pecking order of a family, they are right near the top. I have to admit I have had a better rapport with Harry than any other member of the family.

There is a reason for this.

You can call a dog and when he comes running to your side, you can say, "I don't want anything. I just wanted to know where you are." Try this with a kid and he'll break your knees.

A dog will sit with you through the worst television show in the history of video, and if you like it, never once will he try to change the channel and get something better.

He never entertains friends, forcing you to retire to your bedroom like a felon serving time.

He never lies to you and never gets upset if you don't remember his birthday.

Any relationship is strengthened by a friend who can keep a secret. You tell a dog you don't know what you'll do if you can't come up with the interest on your charge card before the 15th and he'll keep it to himself.

There was a story of a man in Wisconsin who said his wife and his dog did not get along. One of them had to go, so he put an ad in the paper that read, "WIFE OR DOG MUST GO. WIFE IS GOOD-LOOKING BLONDE, BUT IMPATIENT. DOG IS GERMAN SHORTHAIR, 2½ YEARS OLD, SPAYED FEMALE. YOUR CHOICE, FREE."

He received more than twenty calls from people interested in the dog. One caller said he had a short brunette and an English setter and wanted to know if they could swap.

My husband loved that story. He said it made sense. "After all, a dog could give him all the tender loving care his wife could. He could fetch his slippers and newspapers, never hang on the phone all day long or leave dirty dishes soaking in the sink, and would keep his feet warm at night."

I said, "If you feel that way, how come you didn't marry a dog?"

My husband is too smart . . . too old . . . and too well fed to even think of touching that line.

THE GOSPEL OF THE UTILITIES . . . ACCORDING TO DAD

From the kitchen, the voice was barely audible.

"It's coming from the living room," said one son.

We all froze like a tableau.

"Well, excuse me. I didn't realize there was someone still in this room. Silly me. I was ready to turn the lights out. Here, let me turn on a few more lights," the voice continued. "I can afford it. I'm independently wealthy, you know."

I smiled knowingly. "It's your father . . . the 'Prince of Darkness' . . . making a point," I said.

"Don't tell me," said my son, "let me guess. Dad is standing in an empty living room talking to himself to let us know we didn't turn the lights off again when we left the room.''

The other son shook his head. ''Some things never change.''

The speech was a staple. For thirty years Dad had dedicated his life to flipping off lights in rooms with no one in them, turning off water spigots in the bathroom, and throwing his body over the meter in an effort to stop the dials from spinning.

His sermons on saving money and energy fell on deaf ears. His commandments on misuse lay like broken stone tablets amidst the wet towels and melting soap. For more than thirty years, he valiantly fought apathy—alone and unheeded. His gospel of utilities never got the respect he had hoped for.

THOU SHALT FLUSH. ESPECIALLY IF THOU IS FIFTEEN YEARS OLD AND HAS THE USE OF BOTH ARMS.

THOU SHALT HANG UP THE PHONE WHEN THOU HAS BEEN ON IT LONG ENOUGH FOR THE RATES TO CHANGE.

THOU SHALT NOT STAND IN FRONT OF THE REFRIGERATOR DOOR WAITING FOR SOMETHING TO DANCE.

THOU SHALT NOT COVET THE REST OF THE FAMILY'S HOT WATER.

THOU SHALT HONOR THY FATHER'S AND MOTHER'S THERMOSTAT AND KEEP IT ON NORMAL.

THOU SHALT REMEMBER LAST MONTH'S ELECTRICITY BILL AND REJOICE IN DARKNESS.

There were other commandments, but these were the ones written in stone.

He began teaching them when the children were old enough to respond to the word "no."

The phone company didn't make it easy. In the ads they made it look like such a pleasurable experience to talk on the phone. Grandma and Granddad were both poised over the receiver listening to their grandchild burp. Or an entire band jammed in a phone booth to call the tuba player who had to stay at home with his lip in a cast. Sometimes they showed you college friends calling coast to coast with tears in their eyes to describe a western sunset.

Maybe it used to be that way. But that was before Grandma and Granddad realized the burp cost them $9.12. It was before the band cashed in their airline tickets to make the call. Before friends realized it was cheaper to take a bus to see the sunset than to talk about it.

Our phone bill prompted my husband to put together the first of a set of rules for placing long-distance calls in the future.

Before placing the call, go to the bathroom.

Blow your nose and get a drink of water.

Read the weather report of the town you are calling to eliminate, ''What's the weather like?''

Figure out the time zone to conserve conversation on ''What time is it there?''

Don't play games like, ''Guess who this is?''

Fight with your brother BEFORE dialing.

Laughter costs dollars. Save it until you're off the phone.

Don't repeat. If someone says, ''I love you,'' there is no need to say, ''I love you too.'' A simple ''ditto'' will suffice.

Animals and babies are a waste of time on the phone. They never bark/laugh/talk/sing anyway until they hear the party hang up, so write letters.

If you really wanted to see old dad lose it, you should have seen him walk into the kitchen and discover three kids with both doors of the refrigerator flung open while the hairs in their noses froze up. He had a rule for that too. He came up with an idea he used on our safe-deposit box. Every time he'd take out a document for our taxes, he would record it on a little sheet of paper. When he returned an insurance policy or our passports, he would write it down. In one glance, he knew what was in and what was out of the safe-deposit box.

He figured it should work with the refrigerator, so he posted the contents on the refrigerator door and asked the family to mark any withdrawals or additions on the sheet.

A cabbage roll had seven ins and outs, signifying no one knew what it was until he bit into it. Some smart aleck withdrew thirty-five cherries and two peaches and returned thirty-five cherry seeds and two peach pits for inventory. A box of baking soda was withdrawn and returned with a note that said, "Needs work."

Probably the most pathetic entry listed under withdrawals was ice cubes with a note that said, "Would have returned same, but don't know how to make them."

He tried so hard. I used to watch him as he lined the children in front of the door and said, "Today we're going to learn how to speak thermostat. When your room is cold, what do you do?"

One of the boys came forward and hiked the thermostat up to 80.

"You have the idea, but you need a little fine tuning," said his father. "Now, when your room gets too hot, as it will, what do you do?"

"Open a window," yawned our daughter.

They listened intently to his "Daddy is not a rich man" speech and dutifully followed him to the meter so they could watch the little dials twirl around. He told them how much we were charged for each little twirl. I used to feel sorry for him as I watched from a distance, his lips forming the word "bankruptcy."

Finally, one day, one of them said, "Wait a minute. Are you telling us that the colder it gets outside, the harder the furnace has to work to keep it warm inside? And that every time it clicks on it costs money?"

My husband nodded excitedly.

"Then you should have thought of that before you had three children," he said.

At times our home has been mistaken for a nuclear power plant, a site of the premiere of a major motion picture, a night baseball game, or Mardi Gras in progress.

Despite his lectures on how a light switch works, we still have the only "lighthouse" offering a perpetual beacon for sailors adrift in the Arizona desert.

I remember the night we arrived home to find thirty-two lights burning. My husband rousted the family out of bed and ordered them to the dining room, where he shuffled through a stack of papers and figures.

"Did you know," he asked, "that it costs each of us $135 a year to take a hot bath and that the washer costs $3.50 a year to operate?"

"Are you suggesting that we all bathe together in the soak cycle of the washer?" yawned one of the kids.

"I am suggesting that we all take a good look at what is going on around here. A shower is a lot cheaper and uses less water." They thanked him for sharing and got up to leave.

"Sit!" he ordered. "A waterbed costs $4.35 a year to heat, while an electric blanket costs only $2.20."

"Great," said our son, "why don't we all stand under a hair dryer to keep warm. That only costs $1.75 a year.

"For a nickel more," said another son, "we could use the vacuum sweeper to suck the dirt off."

My husband stomped off in defeat.

"Your father has a point," I told the kids. "After all, he pays the bills and all he gets back for it is waste. From here on in, we stop and think about how much it costs in electricity before we turn on a single appliance."

When my husband came to breakfast, he said, "Where's the coffee?"

"I made it in the popcorn popper," said our daughter. "It only costs 40 cents to run, while the electric coffee maker costs $5.40."

One son didn't shave because it cost 40 cents a year. The other one was late for work because the clock ($1.03) was unplugged, and a strange smell was coming from the freezer because it cost $109.45 a year to keep it plugged in.

I offered him a piece of solar toast from the window sill, but he just kept walking toward the door.

It was rather predictable that he would end up talking to himself.

THE FAMILY THAT EATS TOGETHER . . . GETS INDIGESTION

Friday: 7 P.M.

As Yogi Berra once said, "It was déjà vu all over again." One child was throwing plates on the table like a Greek dancer, and one was standing in front of the refrigerator with both doors parted like the Red Sea, whining, "There's nothing to eat."

He was joined by his brother, who said, "You don't know hunger until you're the last kid to leave home. Do you have any idea what I got when all of you left? Every container in the house had a stalk of wheat on it. There were imitation eggs, yogurt cultures multiplying and dividing in the refrigerator like a bad Japanese film, and Civil War milk—blue or gray."

43

"Poor baby," said his sister. "Tell us again how you drove a car to school at sixteen just to keep the battery charged for the old folks."

"They are so health conscious," he continued, "they actually bought sugar-free laxatives. Can you believe that! What did they think I was going to do with it? Pour it over ice cream and pig out?"

"Get out the violins."

"The minute you guys come home for a visit, it's a Pillsbury Dough Boy festival."

"Is he deprived or what?" said his brother.

"You never had to use old encyclopedias where the most recent president was Harry S. Truman," he continued.

"And we didn't get a watch for our twelfth birthday, either," said his brother.

"Just sit on it."

"Lighten up!"

"Give it a rest and help set the table."

"That's woman's work."

"I'm telling! Mom!"

The voices were deeper. The bodies were larger. But the dialogue was from the mouths of the same people who were at the same dinner table fifteen years ago.

It was a performance staged especially for parents. Next to *Chorus Line* and *Oh*! *Calcutta*!, it enjoyed one of the longest runs in the history of modern theater. It was all coming back to me.

* * *

"Mom! Make her stop," said a voice flatly.

The silence was still deafening. "Make her stop what?"

"Humming."

"I don't hear anything."

"You never hear it. She's humming just so no one can hear it but me."

I leaned over, my hair resting on her lips, and listened. Nothing.

"Look at her neck," her brother commanded. "You can see it moving."

I felt her neck to see if the veins were warm. Then I commanded her to stop.

"Did she do it?" I asked my son.

He smiled triumphantly.

Sibling Rivalry was invented by psychoanalyst Alfred Adler in the early 1920s. Up until that time parents used words like "They're killing one another" and "For God's sake, Larry, don't turn your back on 'em." Adler said it was a "phase" children went through in which they competed for their parents' attention. They had it. They just didn't know it.

As the silence of the table returned, I said to the "baby," "Why don't you say a prayer before dinner?"

The other two exchanged knowing glances like the first two cuts in the Miss America pageant.

He bowed his head and began, "Bless us, oh Lord, and these thy gifts which we are about to receive from the Brownies . . ."

"Not Brownies, dork," interrupted his brother. "You mean bounties."

"Bounties is something you get for bringing in an outlaw," said his sister.

"No, you're thinking of the ones who bring in prisoners in Canada. They're Mounties."

"You're thinking of Monty, which was a nickname for General Montgomery during the big war," said their father.

"Monty!" said our daughter. "They were the sisters who wrote *Wuthering Heights* and *Jane Eyre.*"

"That's Brontë," I said.

"I thought Brontë made chicken," he said.

"Jerk, that's Swanson," said his brother.

"No, that's Colonel Sanders, the man with the little white beard and the white suit."

"You are obviously thinking of Mark Twain."

"Wrong," said their father. "It was Mark Clark and he was not a colonel, he was a general during the big war."

"Is he related to Dick Clark?" asked our son.

"Who's Dick Clark?"

"Maybe he's related to Petula Clark."

"What's a Petula?"

"Isn't it like a cuspidor?"

"That's a tooth like a molar."

"A mole is a little animal that ruins your grass."

"No it isn't. It's a little dot on your face that you were born with."

"That is a wart and it's something icky that boys hate but always wind up with."

There was a silence for almost ten seconds when a small voice said, "That's what I said in the first place. Bless these gifts which we are about to receive from the Brownies. . . ."

Sibling rivalry in our family began the first day I brought our second son home from the hospital. His brother looked at him and said, "Maybe later we could get a dog."

The rivalry was subtle at first. Like he'd stand on the baby's windpipe or trap him under the casters of his playpen. At the grocery, he pushed his cart into a blank wall and left him.

"What's with you and your brother?" I'd ask. "He's dumb. He doesn't do anything. He just slobbers and eats the labels off of cans."

It never got any better. When he stopped slobbering, he began to spit. When we got his mouth fixed, his nose started to run. When he walked, he stumbled; when he sat down, he got something wet. Even breathing became annoying.

When children are born, they come equipped with a computer bank that files away every kindness or gift ever rendered and the age it was rendered.

Heaven help the parent who gives one child a bicycle a year sooner than his brother or sister got one, or rewards him with a trip to the circus before the exact hour the others received their first trip to the circus.

The parents are not totally blameless.

I can't think of a mother in this entire world who has not committed the first sin of parenting: comparing her children.

From the day kids are born, we compare them with ourselves, their siblings, their contemporaries, and every other child with whom they come in contact.

They are smaller than their brother when he was that age. They are dumber than their sister in math, lazier than the boy next door, don't catch a baseball like their dad, and their hair doesn't hold the curl like their mother's.

One day my younger son said, "Why do you always compare me to my brother?"

"Because you're a cheap shot," I said.

"I wish I was an only child."

"Wouldn't matter," I said. "When I was carrying your brother, I compared him to a baby my best friend was carrying. Hers moved more than your brother did."

Near the end of the meal, one of them kicked another one under the table. When I asked why, he said, "HE knows." When I asked "He," I was told, "He's lying." When I told him to stop it, he said, "You let him yell 'EEEEEE' at me all the time and never say a word."

It went back and forth like that until the end of the meal.

I told one of them to go to his room. He said, "Sure, he's Mama's favorite."

He was right. Every mother had a favorite. I had mine. It was always the child who was too sick to eat the ice cream at his birthday party, had measles at Christmas, and wore leg braces to bed because he toed in.

She was the fever in the middle of the night, the asthma attack, the child in my arms at the emergency ward.

My "favorite child" was the one I punished for lying, grounded for insensitivity to other people's feelings, and informed was a royal pain to the entire family.

The favorite child said dumb things for which there were no excuses. He was selfish, immature, bad-tempered and self-centered. He was vulnerable, lonely, unsure of what he was doing in this world . . . and quite wonderful.

The one I loved the most was the one I watched struggle . . . and because the struggle was his . . . did nothing.

Every mother knows her favorite child was the one who deserved love the least . . . but needed it the most.

As parents sit and listen to this exchange between siblings at the dinner table, they cannot help but reflect on the dazzling performance. But then the kids have enjoyed a long run with it.

No one asks for an encore, but you get one anyway as they spring into their "It's not my turn to do dishes." Their freshness never ceases to amaze me.

* * *

If a poll were taken of children asking why they thought their parents had children, 12% of them would say they got bored watching television, 26% would say it was a 4-H project that got out of hand, and 62% would swear adults had kids to get out of doing their own dishes.

Despite the fact that fifteen million Americans walk around half sick from eating off of diseased dishes and breakage runs into six figures, it is still the number one chore of kids in the country today.

Early in my mothering career, I saw what I had going for me: a surly child who secretly spit on plates after she rinsed them, laying a foundation of mistrust; a child with kidneys the size of lentils who visited the bathroom five times during the clearing ritual; and another one who argued about it not being his turn for so long the dishes went out of style and the silver pattern was discontinued.

When electric dishwashers came out, I figured it would do for my family what panty hose did for my condo thighs . . . pull them together as one.

The day the dishwasher was installed marked the first time my children fought . . . yes, fought . . . to see who would load it first.

The second night, the one who used to spit on the plates opened the door of the dishwasher and said, ''How do you expect me to clear the table when there are dishes in there from yesterday?''

I had an answer. She did not like it.

"No one said anything about emptying the dishwasher," she said. "I just fill it."

Had this child been a steward on the *Titanic* and someone asked her for a life preserver, she would have said, "I'm sorry, but that is not my station. I work the aft deck."

I cannot put my finger on it, but there was just something "yucky" about touching all those squeaky clean plates and sparkling pieces of silverware and returning them to the drawers and cupboards that turned kids off. They just didn't want to get their hands clean.

I've been emptying the dishwasher ever since we got it. As I do it, I cannot help but reflect on why I had children. What a thing to say. I had them because they would carry my genes and give me everlasting life. They would fill my life with joy and purpose and give meaning to my very existence.

On the other hand, German shepherd puppies can lick a dish clean in 30 seconds without moving the plate . . . and they're real pleasant while they're doing it.

I don't understand it. The kids sit there all during dinner and never mention dishes. The conversation is light. Then one starts with something as subtle as, "Boy, I got a lot of homework tonight. The rest of you can sit here and talk if you want." He begins to leave the table.

"You leave this table," says another sibling,

"and I'll break your face. It's not my turn to do dishes!"

The other one hops in, "It's not my turn. I didn't eat anything, so I'm out."

The first one says, "We can figure this out very simply. I did them Tuesday because we had spaghetti. I always get stuck doing them when we have spaghetti because Mom never liked me."

"Get off my case," says another cast member. "You haven't done them in three weeks because of ball practice. You don't even play ball. You just suit up and sit in the shower room to get out of doing dishes."

"That's a pretty rotten thing to say for someone who lets the dog help him clear. You think we haven't seen you?"

"At least I don't leave the broiler in the oven, the pans soaking in the sink, and save empty corn cobs in the refrigerator."

It's the end of the first act. Parents give them a sitting ovation.

In my naïveté, I always thought a family doing dishes together built character. I perceived it as a sharing experience where everyone pitched in and made it a better world.

This myth exploded the night we took a steak knife away from one of the boys who said it wasn't his "turn" and was using his brother as a dart board.

We moved right along to plan B, in which each of them would have his night in the kitchen and then be off for two nights. However, there was so much trading and paying back that the bookkeeping became unwieldy and we moved to a new house to start fresh.

We called the kids the three S's. Each had his own personality in the kitchen.

One was a Soaker. Everything soaked. The only thing that wasn't put in the sink and filled with water was the spaghetti pot, which always looked clean and hung with spaghetti hardened on it for three years.

One was a Saver. No leftover was too small to store in its original serving dish: a grape, a French fry, a wad of gum left on the dinner plate. All were preserved for whoever was on for dishes the next night.

The other one was a Slammer . . . a one-person wrecking crew who could demolish a table in 30 seconds. She cleared. She stacked. She washed. She dried. She put away. All of this in fifteen seconds and at great expense to the management.

All three, however, had one trait in common. The moment the meal was over, a biological urgency would come over them and they would disappear into the bathroom until they were sure the food on the plates was in a solid state.

It was a game they played. Would Mom sigh her martyrdom sigh and say, "Never mind, I'll do them myself," and when they emerged from the bathroom the kitchen would be sparkling and the dishes done?

Or would Mom fake 'em out and they would be in the kitchen giving a prime time performance to no one?

It was an act that was always held over. Yet, to this day they can't hear a dish rattle without instinctively going into the bathroom and locking the door.

WHO KILLED THE HOME-COOKED McMEAL?

In retrospect, it was only a matter of time before the Family Dinner Hour passed into history and fast foods took over. I knew its days were numbered the day our youngest propped my mouth open with a fork and yelled into it, "I want a cheeseburger and two fries and get it right this time." I just didn't serve meals with show business pizzazz.

My pot roast gave way to pizza served in a derby hat and cane. My burgers couldn't compete with the changing numbers under the Golden Arches. I couldn't even do chicken . . . right!

So, day by day I watched the family go outside of the home for meals where there were no tables to set and no clean hands required, and where green was not considered a happy color. The warm smells of Mother's kitchen gave way to the back seat of a station wagon littered with supermarket flyers, dry cleaning, schoolbooks, ropes, chains, jumper cables, and dog hairs.

The old rules for eating at home—sit up straight, chew your food, and don't laugh with cottage cheese in your mouth—didn't fit the new ambiance. A new set of rules emerged.

When ordering from the back seat of the car, do not cup your mouth over Daddy's ear and shout into it. Wait quietly until you are asked what you want. Follow this with "thank you."

Never order more than you can balance between your knees. Remember, ice that spills between your legs dampens not only spirit . . . as it were. If by some chance you receive a sandwich that is not yours, do not spit on it and throw it on the floor. Simply pass it back to the driver of the car and tell him a mistake has been made.

Front-of-the-car seating is better than back seat if you have a choice. The dashboard offers space for holding beverages. However, these are reserved for parents who have seniority in the family.

Conversation while dining in a car should be restricted to school happenings, future social events, and a polite exchange about noncontroversial issues. It is quite improper to carry on a discourse as to what the secret sauce reminds you of.

Eat with your legs together at all times. Unless

the car windows are tinted, there should be no physical exchange between diners in the back seat.

Remember, you are basically dining in public. That means no French fries hung from the nose. Very few diners will find this amusing. Despite the fact that facilities in the car are limited, there is no reason why it should be a major McMess. Afterward, each person should be responsible for his/her trash and should contain it in a bag. Two-week-old onion rings in the ashtray are not a pretty sight.

Why did the home-cooked meal become extinct? Maybe because it deserved to die. I got to the point where I couldn't even get the family to the table at one time. When I announced, "Dinnnner!" the entire family swung into action like a precision drill team of Viennese Lippizaners. For no apparent reason, my husband would exit to the bathroom with two volumes on Churchill, one child would pick up the telephone and dial a random number, another would grab a basketball and go outside to shoot baskets, and one of them would take a bus somewhere.

When Donna Reed first invented the dinner hour, it was designed to be a gathering place for the family, where they would sit around and exchange pleasantries about the asparagus.

Our family, when we got together, sounded like we were attending a lynching.

The problem at family dinners is that no one can agree on what is considered to be a "fit topic to discuss at dinner time." Children tend to talk about things that take away your interest in food—and living. At one meal alone, I heard a description of the underside of the tongue, a rumor of what popular food contained rats' nostrils, what pureed peas remind you of when you look at them from a distance, and what happens to a dog's stool when he eats leftover chicken.

Men prefer to talk about money. Within minutes they can make you feel guilty for asking for seconds on the salt. They also take the opportunity to lay on the family their famous lectures on ''An 'E' on the gas gauge does not mean evacuate,'' ''Don't reach out and touch somebody unless it's collect,'' and my all-time favorite, ''Why do we have to straighten his teeth? He never smiles anyway.''

Mothers use the togetherness of the meal to discuss the sins children committed in their diapers. (''No one ever amounted to anything who made a bed with a coat hanger.'')

As a cook, I don't know how much longer I could have endured the eating habits of my family. I discovered the more teeth the kid had, the less he chewed. They never ate anything that was green or was contained in a sack with their name on it. They never ate the same cereal twice and believed in their hearts that the dog got better food than they did.

Eventually, even my husband and I were seduced by the convenience of dining out. No wonder I loved it. I had never seen so many people in my life before. As we drove up to a restaurant with our friends, a valet opened our car door and said, "Hi, my name is Hal and I'll park your car. Have a good dinner."

I said, "Thank you, Hal. I'm Erma and this is my husband, Bill, and our friends, Dick and Bernice."

Inside, after we were seated, a young woman appeared and said, "Good evening. My name is Wendy, and I'm your cocktail waitress. What could I get you this evening?"

I introduced all of us again and we ordered something from the bar. My husband leaned over and said, "So, Dick, what's happening?"

A waiter brought a basket of bread to our table and said, "Good evening, folks. I'm Brick and these are our special toasted garlic rounds with just a hint of Parmesan and fresh parsley. If you need more, yell. Enjoy."

"Thanks, Brick," my husband said. "So, what's happening, Dick?"

Another waiter appeared and said, "Hello, I'm Stud and I'll be your waiter for this evening. I'd like to interrupt for just a minute to tell you about our specials this evening. The chef has prepared osso buco. This is made from knuckle of veal, garlic, chicken sauce, white wine, tomato paste, and anchovy fillets finely chopped.

"The catch of the day is smoked cod's roe, which the chef makes into tarama salata smothered with black olives, heavy cream, lemon, and olive oil.

"The soup of the day is everyone's favorite, watercress and apple, with just a pinch of curry. I'll give you a minute to decide."

Numbly, we looked at one another. His monologue had lasted longer than most marriages.

"So, Dick, what's happening with you?" my husband began again.

Wendy reappeared and said, "Refills, anyone?"

We shook our heads.

Stud followed her to the table and said, "Are we ready to order now?"

No sooner had Dick and Bernice agreed to share the salad than a table appeared and Stud narrated the drama of the birth of a Caesar salad like a midwife.

Meanwhile, Frank (the chef) appeared with a naked fish, which he stuck under my nose for approval. (Thank God I didn't order the strangled duck!) After the salad table came another table with flames leaping off it, and Stud electrified us with his commentary on sauce for the Moroccan meatballs.

Arthur appeared with a key around his neck and a book that weighed 36 pounds and introduced himself as our wine steward. I introduced him to Bill, Dick, and Bernice.

When the entrées were placed before us, no one dared touch his food until he had gone through the Black Pepper Experience. Now, I don't pretend to understand when pepper got to be right up there behind frankincense and myrrh, but it is. That's when Stud came over to the table with a pepper mill the size of a piano leg (the bigger the pepper mill . . . the larger the check) and said, "Pepper?"

All the conversation came to a halt while we thought about what our answers would be when it came to us. I hesitated a moment and then said, "Yes, please." Stud watched my hand, waiting for me to orchestrate how much and the precise moment to stop.

The weird part of this is that *not one grain of pepper* comes out of the mill. (It's sorta like watching the first piece of luggage come off a carousel in airport baggage. Ever see anyone claim it? Of course you haven't. Because it doesn't belong to anyone, that's why.)

As Brick cleared the table, Stud appeared with his dessert cart and Wendy pouted openly when no one wanted a liqueur. I wanted coffee, but if we stayed any longer, I'd have been too old to lift the cup.

We said good-bye to Hal, Wendy, Brick, Stud, Frank, and Arthur. We were exhausted.

I suppose someday the home-cooked meal may return. When? Maybe when they come out with Phyllis Diller's fantasy: a stove that flushes. Who knows?

As one of the kids rummaged in the refrigerator, he said, "What's this?"

"It's celery and it's good for you."

He said, "If it's so great, then how come it never danced on television?"

I couldn't answer him.

TECHNOLOGY'S COMING . . . TECHNOLOGY'S COMING

Friday: 8 P.M.

The younger son made his move first. He jumped up from the table and said, "I've gotta get my laundry started or I can't go out. What time is it?"

I looked at my watch. "It's 6 A.M. in Hamburg, Germany, if that helps."

"Why do you know the time in Hamburg, Mom?"

"Because that is where the watch was made and set and the directions for resetting it are written in German."

"The clock on the oven says it's 11."

"That's wrong," said my husband. "Your mother can't see what she's twirling half the time

63

without her glasses and sometimes when she sets the timer, she resets the clock.''

''And the one on the VCR?'' he asked.

''. . . is always 12 and blinking,'' I said, ''because your father screwed up between steps two and five when the power went out.''

''God, Mom, you and Dad are out of it. It's like the *Twilight Zone*. How do you two function around here? I'd be lost without technology. This little beeper,'' he said, patting his shirt pocket, ''keeps me in touch with the world.''

''He's right, Mom,'' said our daughter, ''you oughta have one of those signals attached to your car keys and your glasses. Think of the time you could save.''

It was a subject I hated.

''Maybe we should have tranquilized you with a dart and fitted you with a beeper to track your migratory habits when you were seventeen and we'd have all slept better,'' I snapped.

''Mom, why do you resist the twenty-first century? You don't even have a home computer.''

''I don't need a home computer. What would I do with it?''

''A lot of things. You could store all your personal documents in one place . . . your marriage license, your insurance policies, your warranties. Just think, you and Dad could punch up your insurance policies in seconds.''

''We could die from the excitement,'' I said.

''You could even use a copier around here,''

piped in her brother, "to duplicate all of our medical records and your dental bills, not to mention a Christmas newsletter."

"We need a copier like the Osmonds need a cavity fighter," I said.

"She's hopeless," they shrugged.

I sat there alone, toying with my coffee. They had told me what I didn't want to hear. Their father and I were casualties in the war of automation. Why did we resist it? Maybe because there was a time when there weren't enough hours in the day to fulfill all the skills of my job description. I was chauffeur, cook, nurse, decorator, financier, psychologist, and social director. I was important. All the slick magazines said so.

Slowly but steadily I was replaced by beeps, switches, flashing lights, electronic devices, and monotone voices.

In the beginning, I taught my children how to tie their shoes and button and zip their clothing. Then along came Velcro tabs on their shoes and on their clothes where buttons and zippers used to be.

I used to tell them how to place an emergency call to Grandma if they needed her. Now it was a matter of pushing a button on a memory phone and it was done for them.

I used to enlighten them about the stove. I showed them how to turn it on and off so they wouldn't get burned. They don't have stoves anymore. They have microwave ovens that have little buttons to push and are cool to the touch.

At one time I pulled them on my lap and together we traced our fingers across the printed page as I read to them. I don't read anymore. All they have to do is insert book cassettes into their stereos and hear them read by professionals.

I have been replaced by ouchless adhesive bandages, typewriters that correct their spelling, color-coded wardrobes, and computers that praise them when they get the right answers. The future is here.

The kids are wrong. It isn't that we don't give technology a chance. We use the VCR. True, it was in our home for a full six months before we turned it on.

From time to time my husband would leaf through the manual with an intensity usually reserved for a nervous flier reading about the evacuation procedures on an aircraft. Then one day he said, "Since we are going out to dinner, I am going to tape *Dallas* so we can watch it later."

I put my hand over his. "I want you to know that whatever happens, I think you're the bravest man I have ever met."

Looking back, that was the beginning of our march against time.

There are 24 hours in every day. I used to watch television 6 hours and 44 minutes a day, leaving me with 17 hours and 16 minutes.

After I scheduled 7 hours and 5 minutes to sleep and 2 hours and 15 minutes to eat, it only left me with 7 hours and 56 minutes to do my job.

Then we got cable television and what with the

news channel, first-run movies, MTV, country western, spiritual, entertainment, and sports, my viewing cut into my workday. The VCR was supposed to solve our problem.

But when do you watch the shows you've taped?

I took time away from my 2 hours and 15 minutes eating time by eating in front of the TV set. Naturally, we began to buy cassettes to fit the VCR. I bought Jane Fonda so I could get my body into shape. However, I had to take time away from my 7 hours and 5 minutes of sleeping to do it.

On my birthday, a son rented two movies as a present. I panicked. They had to be viewed by 10 A.M.. the next morning. Already I had a stack of shows that had been taped that I hadn't had time to view. I put the movies ahead of the tapes, rescheduled Jane Fonda for 4 A.M., and watched *Terms of Endearment* and *Easy Money* at 5 and 7 A.M. It was close but I made it.

Other scheduling problems were not so easily solved. Before dinner one night, I approached the VCR with my Julia Child cassette. My husband was watching Dan Rather. When I asked him to watch Dan in the bedroom, he said it wouldn't do any good as he was taping a *M*A*S*H* rerun on the other channel. I went into the kitchen, turned on another set, and watched *Wheel of Fortune*, and we didn't eat until 9:30 in front of *Magnum P.I.*

As the weeks go on, I feel the pressure more and more. With the VCR taping shows day and night, with my husband running from room to room, channel-searching to see what we're missing, the new cassettes on everything from how to repair your plumbing to how to be more assertive, the new films and video music, we're falling behind.

Already we're beginning to cut corners. We've got *60 Minutes* down to 30, *20/20* to 10/10, and anything on World War II we fast-forward because we know the ending.

But the cassettes are winning. We both know that. It's only a matter of time.

Our son returned to the kitchen with his father's running watch in his hand. "I don't believe you, Dad. You've been telling time by your memory/recall lap 4, total time. Here, let me show you how it works. You've got a multimode chronograph and multimode countdown timer with one-tenth second accuracy."

I watched the two of them hunched over the watch as my son patiently explained the mechanism.

Had it been twenty-some years since they had huddled over the kitchen table together and my husband brought forth the brand-new watch for his son and taught him how to tell time? They had "walked through" all the parts when they got down to the basics. When the big hand pointed toward the refrigerator and the small hand was toward the stove, it was 6 o'clock and time to eat. When the big hand was toward the mixer and the little hand was pointed toward the portable television set, it was time to go to bed.

If the kid went into a home or building where the furniture was not positioned in the same spot as our kitchen, he was to go to the nearest person and ask, "What time is it?"

With deft fingers, our son twisted dials and adjusted minute screws on the watch. My husband watched with admiration and awe. He had come a long way since that day twenty years ago at the kitchen table.

Minutes later, "Mr. Technology" yelled from the utility room, "Mom, how do you turn the washer on?"

Maybe not.

" 'NO PESTS?'
I THOUGHT IT SAID
'NO PETS' "

Where did I fail?

No one could accuse me of not trying to domesticate our children to feed and to care for themselves. But face it, they led sheltered lives under our roof. They never saw a naked chicken, never assisted at the birth of a casserole, or walked in unexpectedly and viewed the resuscitation of bread dough.

The harder I tried to educate them, the more they regarded the kitchen as an "adult community" that did not accept children or pets. Their visits were limited to throwing open the freezer/refrigerator doors and declaring, "There's nothing to eat in this house."

I cannot tell you the number of times I tried to

lure them into the kitchen with teasers like, "Have you no curiosity as to how the cereal gets into the bowl?" or "Come. Stand by my side and together we will 'just add water.' " Once when I made my son watch as I mixed a Caesar salad, he looked at the oil, bits of garlic, lemon juice, Worcestershire sauce, Parmesan, and a raw egg floating in the bowl and said, "That's gross" and walked away.

Take the kid in the utility room pushing every button in sight. Did I not try to share with him my years of experience? "You have to have patience for a 'sparkling wash,' " I told him. "Wet is just not good enough." For twenty minutes once, I shared with him the ecstasy of burying your face in a stack of clean underwear. You'd have thought I was giving him instructions on how to fuel a nuclear reactor. He said he was against it and he didn't want to bring his children into a world of bleach.

Kids just have a different set of priorities for their life-styles. Traditionally, when their parents got their first apartment, it looked like a stripped-down version of the home they just left. Today's generation is different.

If there are no plugs in the bathroom? They don't care.

If the room isn't wired for heating? They don't care.

If the front door doesn't close? They don't care.

If there's a commune of bikers living next door? They don't care.

If the stove doesn't work? They don't care.

If there are two large walls that will hold the weight of their speakers, they'll rent it.

I remember the first time we visited our son's apartment.

I stood at the door numbly. It was minutes before I realized that I had just handed my coat to a cockroach who hung it up on the curtain rod in the shower.

My eyes scanned his room. A sofa with a single sheet and a blanket. A card table with four folding chairs. Two cereal bowls, three spoons, a phone with a 50-foot cord, and a $4,000 stereo.

I opened up his refrigerator door. On the first shelf was a container half full of yogurt. On the second shelf was a roll of film and a hardened lime. A doggie bag in the meat keeper was later identified as sweet and sour pork.

How did it happen that I raised three children who never picked up anything but a fork?

Somewhere between boiling the pacifier and buying black towels, I lost 'em. I don't know how or why, but I unleashed upon society three kids who think self-cleaning bathrooms have already been invented.

What really frosts me is that it reflects on me. You have to believe me when I say, they weren't raised this way. I use soap when I do dishes. I don't wear a shirt the fourth day by turning it wrong-side-out. I do not store Slushee cups under the gas pedal. I do not sleep on pillows that have no cases on them, nor have I ever drunk milk out of a carton. Before every meal I used to ask, "Did you wash your hands and face?"

In reply, a 24-inch tongue came out of their mouths and, like a street cleaner, made a path, bordered on the north by a nose, east and west by cheeks, and on the south by a chin. A simple "no" would have done it.

You're looking at a woman who, for years, declared all-out war on her children's bedrooms. I had to. Baby-sitters would demand medical benefits before coming to sit. I couldn't set a full table without visiting their rooms.

A psychologist I admired said parents made too much of things and reacted too strongly. All I had to do was lay out a situation, then praise the child for it. For example, if a child left a book on the floor, all I had to say was, "There's a book on the floor," and he would arrive at the decision of what should be done with it. The child would be in control, not me.

To test the theory, I put a book on the floor and said to the first child to arrive, "There's a book on the floor." He said "I know. I nearly broke my neck tripping over it. Better pick it up," and disappeared. The second one came by and when I told him of the book said, "You're real swift today."

I got so disgusted, I didn't try it with the third one.

Still, his turn came. One day after I viewed his

bedroom, I thought I should give him the chance to redeem himself.

When he asked me to go to a movie with him, I said, "I'd love to go to the movie with you, but I have to do all the work you didn't do today."

There was genuine concern written all over his face. "How much more do you have to do?" he asked.

"There's your dirty clothes all over the floor, your dirty dishes under the bed to take out, your bed to make, your trash to be disposed of, your wet towels to take to the laundry room, and your floor to be vacuumed."

"Hey Mom," he said, "I think I know where you're coming from. Why don't you just get up earlier tomorrow morning and do it?"

The way he lived today shouldn't have been a surprise. After dinner he said, "Don't bother with the dishes. I'll put them in the dishwasher."

I said, "You don't have a dishwasher."

He said, "Of course I do. It's under the stove."

"That's an oven," I said.

He shrugged and said, "No wonder the glasses have spots."

My husband finally could keep quiet no longer. "What's with the roaches?"

"You mean Stewart? I'm working with him to enter him in the Largest Roach in America contest."

"I've never seen one hang up a coat before," I conceded.

"I don't know," said my husband. "You don't know anything about him. Suppose he used to travel with a German girls' Olympics swim team and had access to steroids."

"Or maybe he posed nude for *National Geographic* when he was younger and needed money," I said.

"On the other hand," said his father, "he could walk off with Miss Congeniality and a doughnut endorsement."

Our son looked at us. "Are you two putting me on? Because there is a prize of $1,000."

"That's different," said my husband. "If you won, you could fog this whole place and claim your own bed again."

We talked about it on the way home. Actually, the cockroach and our son had a lot in common. They both came out at night, ate cold fast food, and knew how to empty a room.

Still, their relationship seemed unnatural.

In retrospect, I've learned a lot about kids on their own since the first one peeled off. You never drop in on them unless you have a nitroglycerin tablet ready to slip under your tongue. It is possible to maintain a rapport with them and still know where the dog eats and what a quart of milk is doing on the back of the commode. Just give them four to six weeks' notice before visiting.

You never ask to see the $88 wool afghan you brought them from Ireland unless you're prepared to see it after they washed it in hot water, tossed it in the dryer, and are now using it for a coaster.

Resist the temptation to bring their apartment up to health standards. It will only cause you pain when you return in a few months and find everything as it was before you cleaned it.

I know a lot of parents who get very discouraged. There is one thought that keeps me going. One of these days they will have children of their own.

Come to think of it, it's the only thing.

"YOU SHOULD HAVE GONE BEFORE YOU LEFT HOME"

Friday: 8:30 P.M.

It was my fourth trip to the garage since one son had transferred the snake from the utility room to the hood of my car. This time I had three phone books to add to the top of the cage.

"Whatya doin', Mom?" asked his owner. "You giving these phone books the pitch?"

"They're for the snake," I said.

"Trust me when I tell you he doesn't know a soul in town to call."

"That's not funny. I'm making sure he doesn't escape."

"Jeez," he gasped, "you already have a bag of cement, two 50-pound weights from the weight bench, and a car battery on top of the cage. If it ever caves in, you'll kill him, and every time you try on a pair of pumps in I. Magnin, you'll wonder if it was 'your son's friend.' "

"I don't know why you are doing this to me," I whined, "you know how terrified I am of snakes. Remember that time we stopped by the road in Michigan on vacation? I was a nervous wreck."

He sat on the garbage can with his feet drawn up under his chin. "We sure had some 'interesting' times on vacations, didn't we? That summer in Maine . . . and that dude ranch in Indiana. It was always good for you and Dad to get away, I guess, but it was sure tough on us kids. We had to sit there in the back seat like statues afraid to breathe. We couldn't talk. We couldn't move. Just ride. The three of us cramped together like sardines used to envy you and Dad laughing and talking with nothing to do but ride and read the road map. Remember?"

Remember? I was not likely to forget the hitchhiker who, after 20 miles, wrote us a check to let him out of the car. God, how I envied him. Those trips were like death marches.

A lot of families play games in the car to pass the time, like "Count the Cows" or "Out-of-State License Bingo." Our children played a game called, "Get Mama." It was a 400-mile nonstop argument that began in the driveway and didn't end until I threatened to self-destruct. Through scenic highways, majestic mountains, and amber waves of grain, they argued.

They argued for 75 miles on whether or not you could run a car 100 miles in reverse without stalling. They debated how workers in the U.S. Treasury Department could defraud the detectors by putting $100 bills in their mouths and not smiling until they got past security. They argued about whether or not you could use a yo-yo on the moon and whether or not hair would grow over a vaccination. They discussed at length what if a nun were allowed to become a priest, would you call her "Father"?

They threatened to "slap" a minimum of 55 times and "punch" 85 times, said "I'm telling" 149 times, and whispered, "I'll give you one where it hurts" too many times to count.

The only bright spot I can ever remember was once when I slumped against the door and it wasn't closed all the way and I nearly fell out.

It amazes me how every year, a childless writer will set down suggestions on the joys of traveling with children.

One article I read recommended you "put pillows, snacks, a change of clothes, and some of the children's favorite toys inside the car where they can be easily reached.

"Plan for rest stops about every two hours and, if possible, take a brief walk on these stops.

"Once back on the road, talk about what they saw and did during each stop.

"Use your imagination for other kinds of entertainment. Play guessing games and sing songs."

Well, if that doesn't make you want to go right out and rent a child for your next trip . . . nothing will.

But you're not talking to an amateur. I have traveled with children for the last twenty years and have been in three rest homes and two encounter groups, have written fifteen letters to Dale Evans asking for spiritual guidance, and was in analysis two years after I admitted abandoning a ten-year-old in a roadside gift shop. I have a few suggestions of my own.

The pillow is a great idea. The first one who whines, "Make him stop looking at me," gets it . . . right over the face.

As for commercial games and toys, forget 'em. Children usually like to make up their own. In addition to "Get Mama," there's "Name That Thud!" With her head turned toward the window, Mom has to guess what is making Robbie cry out in pain. There's "Window Roulette" where all the bodies in the back seat are airborne trying to get a seat by the two windows. Other cars will often slow down to watch this one.

I personally like "Statue," a takeoff on the old summer game where Mom reaches over the back seat, gives each a rap, and no matter what position a child lands in, he must remain that way for the next 200 miles.

If you encourage a child to share with you his observations of the last pit stop, be prepared to hear language from a rest room wall that will make your radiator boil over.

Frankly, I have some questions about jamming a family into a car together for a couple of weeks in pursuit of happiness. It has been explained to me a thousand times, but I still don't understand why it is that men feel obliged to start a vacation at four in the morning.

I mean, what good are breathtaking colors of the Smoky Mountains in the dark? How can you feel the pulse and excitement of New York City when a passed-out wino is the only thing on the street? What good is a vacation if you can't keep awake through lunch?

We were the first family ever to "See America First" by headlights. Every morning before hitting the road, we would be awakened by the sound of the alarm going off in the middle of the night. Picking my way through the darkness, I'd guide arms and legs through clothes. It was like threading a needle with wet spaghetti. As the kids continued to sleep, I'd walk them to the car and arrange them in the back seat.

They never awoke asking, "Where are we?" It was always, "What time is it?" They could never play games other children played, like "Count the Chevys" or "Out-of-State License Plate Rummy." There weren't any cars on the road.

We'd sit there like zombies, listening to the hog and grain markets on the car radio, trying to figure out which meal we would spoil if we ate a candy bar.

Once we stopped at a roadside park for a potty break, and I hooked my sweater over the hood ornament to keep from falling down. About the same time, a station wagon pulled in with another family. They looked terrible. The kids stumbled along with blankets dragging on the ground, their hair uncombed, their eyes puffy and glazed. The woman and I didn't say anything at first. Our eyes met in that rare moment of understanding; there was no need to speak. Finally I whispered, "Courage, Sister!" I think of her often.

I wondered if she married a man who regarded asking for directions anywhere as a genetic weakness. I wish I had a dime for every cloverleaf we circled for eight days. "Dear," I'd suggest, "why don't you ask directions from someone?"

"Because I am not lost," he would say. "That's the difference between men and women. Women don't like to figure things out. As soon as they see a cow in a field they panic and right away start asking directions."

It was only the first of many trips where we wandered aimlessly about the countryside, too lost to last . . . and too proud to ask.

We explored every dead-end road in the United States, blazed trails where only covered wagons had been, and discovered maternity homes for bloodsucking mosquitoes.

I wondered if she too married a man with kidneys the size of basketballs who never felt the need for a bladder stop. Whenever I broached the subject, I was always told, "You're bored. You need something to do. Why don't you figure out where we are?"

In truth, I stopped reading road maps in 1977 when my husband accused me of moving the Mississippi River over two states.

It wasn't the first time he yelled at me for tampering with locations. We once quarreled over whether a prominent arch was a McDonald's or the gateway to St. Louis. Another time we had an ugly scene when I wrapped my gum in the Great Lakes and we couldn't find our way to the Canadian border.

Reading road maps is like being a vice president. You wear navy and keep your mouth shut. The only time you are consulted is when the driver is approaching a fork in the road at 55 mph and shouts, "OK, you wanted to drive . . . now which way do we turn?"

It's funny, but the anatomy of our life together can be summed up in the road map experience.

The first year of our marriage, I told my husband I got nauseated when I read in a moving car and he laughed and said, "Sweetheart, I don't want you to do anything but just sit there and talk to me. Just leave the driving to me."

A few years later, when we had three children fighting over two car windows, he started to delegate things for me to do. One was to "keep those kids from killing one another."

A few years later, he added, "Entertain them or give them a sedative."

Then one day he said, "Start looking for the turnoff." When I said I didn't know what turnoff he was talking about, he said, "Look in the glove compartment for the map. It's marked."

"You know I get nauseated when I read in a moving car," I said.

For the next ten years, I was never to see another monument, scenic wonder, Stuckey's, cathedral, sunset, or spacious sky. I sat for hours hunched over a mural of wavy lines, little circles, numbers too small to read, and distances too long to care.

I was to discover road maps made people say things they did not mean.

"We missed Fort Lauderdale. That's what I'd expect from a woman whose mother swims out to meet troop ships."

"Oh sure, I'll get in the left lane . . . when you get out of the sack in the morning and make my breakfast, I'll get in the left lane."

"So which way do I go, Erma? Left or right? I'll give you a hint. You pat the dog with your left hand. You dry your fingernails out of the car window with your right."

It's been ten years since I stuffed a road map up his nose. Ten years of riding in silence. That is not to say there is peace in the back seat of the car. Children do not go on a vacation to have a good time. If parents really wanted them to have a good time, they would leave them at home. Each rebels in his or her own way.

No self-respecting family would think of going on a vacation without the "Seat Kicker." The Seat Kicker is a forerunner of the bionic leg. He positions himself just behind Daddy's seat and has been clocked at 200 kicks per minute for as long as 400 miles. The motion affects his hearing.

And not to be missed is the child we call the "Hysteria Connection." You have just turned onto the freeway when she leans over to where Daddy is smiling in anticipation of a week without pressure and says, "Did you mean to leave the garden hose running, Daddy?" Daddy will not smile again on the trip.

She hears a strange knock in the engine that was the same knock her friend, Robin, heard just before the transmission went out of their car. She hears a newscast issuing tornado warnings for the place you are headed. She notes that the farther you go, the higher the price of gasoline gets, and her asthma seems to be getting worse and she probably will not be able to breathe in the cabin you have rented.

Occasionally, she turns to her brother and asks, "Did you tell Mom about the cat you have hiding under your bed?" or to her sister, "Everyone who's been accepted to State next fall has been notified by now."

She hears sirens before anyone else in the car

and smells burning rubber. She reassures her mother that the Ryans' dog had a hysterectomy and she got fat, too!

And just when you think the Hysteria Connection has dispensed all the good news a family can stand on a vacation, she says, "I didn't want to mention it, but when Daddy was hiding the key under the flowerpot by the door, I saw a man watching him from a parked car across the street." Then she adds cheerfully, "I wouldn't worry. I've been exposed to measles and if I'm on schedule, the rash should appear tonight and we should all be coming home tomorrow."

All of this makes you wonder why you cleaned out the fireplace, sucked the dust out from under the freezer, glued the tile down in the bathroom, fluffed up all the pillows, bought new underwear for the entire family, and ate three black bananas before the house-sitter came. Maybe to give your kids something "interesting" to remember.

THE IDES OF MAY

Friday: 9 P.M.

Throughout the years it has come to be known simply as the "closet experience."

Kids haven't been home unless they've pawed through their old sports trophies and ribbons, 2,080 friendship pictures from grade school, rubber worms, dolls with no eyes, graduation tassels, rugs from Disneyland, pennants, report cards, sand-filled cameras, basketballs, kites, dog-eared letters, college catalogs, and license plates.

It was a monument to another myth. As parents, we had always been led to believe that you didn't lose a daughter or a son to an apartment . . . you gained a closet. When our children were younger, sometimes my husband and I would sneak into their bedrooms as they slept. We would gaze into their closets as I squeezed his hand and smiled, "Just think, Dear . . . one day all of that will be yours." We fantasized about the time each of us would have a rod of our own for our clothes . . . a shelf without Christmas decorations . . . floor space without boxes marked RAIN-SOAKED HALLOWEEN MASKS AND LUCKY GYM SHOES.

It never happened. Their apartments were too small to hold their treasures so they stored them at home and visited them with some regularity.

"What are you digging for?" I asked, wading through a room of boxes and old tennis rackets without strings.

"God Mom, you didn't throw away my baseball cards, did you? They're worth a fortune. Do you have any idea what you can get for a Pete Rose with a burr haircut?"

"She threw away a box of my albums which would have been classics and snatched up by Sotheby's," said his brother.

"You don't know that," I said.

"Mom! *The lyrics were clean!*"

"All I know is I'm sick of saving all this mess. I feel like Miss Havisham in *Great Expectations*, watching the mice nip at the wedding cake."

"Mom, this is our history. It shows that we were here."

"Your father and I live at a poverty level. What more proof do we need that you were here? Why don't both of you just toss some of this stuff out on this visit? Just make a little stack here by the door and I'll get rid of it. I mean it!''

A couple of hours later, I wandered in the room to turn off the lights. A pathetic little stack of memorabilia was mounded by the door. On top was a royal blue graduation gown and a mortarboard with the tassel of the school colors. Our first high school graduate.

What a year that was. No matter how much we budgeted, no one could have prepared us for the Ides of May. No one ever told us that in May, your child wakes up in the morning with her hand outstretched, and every sentence is prefaced by ''I need.''

The education that you thought was free back in September isn't. ''I need $12 for a book I lost.'' ''I need $6 for a ticket for the baseball play-offs.'' ''I need $3 for a present for Miss Weems, who is retiring.'' ''I need your gas card and your car to drive to a party.'' ''I need $40 to sand a desk that someone who looks like me carved my name on.''

The kid who dressed like a wino for twelve years suddenly has a social life which requires a wardrobe. ''I need heels for senior dress-up day.'' ''I need makeup for the class picture even though I'm in the last row.'' ''I need a dress for awards day.''

Parents who support a high school graduate in the final days of May should be eligible for graduation relief benefits. Before you kick in for a senior send-off, you better be sure he or she is going. ''I need a car of my own to show everyone my parents love me." "I need a $200 suit to wear under a graduation gown." "I need a yearbook." "I need $100 to go to dinner before the prom." "I need rental fees for my tux." "I need money for flowers."

"I need money for graduation pictures." The pictures are delivered in April. By June, the cap and gown have been stuffed in a closet. The diploma is jammed in the back of the baby book. The film of the graduation is in the camera and will remain there until the birth of the graduate's first child. The embossed thank-you notes are lost.

There is only one reminder left of that glorious day when your child filled you with such pride: 192 friendship pictures.

When your child ordered 200 of them in February, you would have thought he would have mentioned that he only had eight friends, but not a word was said. How could you possibly have known he was such a loser?

How do you unload 192 friendship pictures? Those of us with a cheap ethic can get pretty creative. I began by sending them to anyone who had ever spoken to me or looked at me like he wanted to speak to me. I sent them to strangers in the phone book who had our same last name. I sent them to creditors, like the gas and phone companies, with my check. For a while I used them as tips. ("Remember young man, there's more where these came from.") I pasted them on the back of my letters and inked PRESERVE WILDLIFE underneath. I stuck them to the back of rest room doors with our phone number underneath.

Eventually, some of them were preserved in plastic to become coasters, and several of them found their way as a border around a bathroom mirror.

I took one out of my billfold and wrapped my gum in it one day. My luncheon companion was shocked. She had no idea I had seventy-eight of them left.

"I need money for a class ring." Every year, millions of class rings are ordered by millions of high school graduates. Yet no one ever sees them. What happens to them?

Class rings are what are lost before your check for them clears the bank. They are what you take off every time you wash your hands the first week you have them . . . and after that are never seen again.

Class rings are what make the strange noises in your washing machine and what you paid $35 to a washer repairman to retrieve under the pulsator. They are what you wear to bed and your hand swells and everyone gives you advice on how to get them off and when you lather up your hands with soap, they fall in the commode.

Class rings (belonging to boys) are what dangle from chains in cleavages of girls as a promise to spend the rest of your life together . . . if you go to the same college.

Class rings (belonging to girls) dangle from the

first knuckle of the baby finger of boys who say they'll wear them forever and are later found in their gym bag.

Class rings are what multiply, grow feet, and appear in the knife and fork drawer, the sewing basket, tied to the blind cord, and in the corner of the bathtub.

Sometimes they turn green.

"I need money for the prom." In the movies, it's always a big scene. The boy picking up the girl for the prom will have a box containing a corsage in his hand. He's standing at the bottom of the stairway looking awkward and uncomfortable talking with the girl's parents.

Suddenly, she appears. Their "little girl" has emerged from her pigtails and jeans into a woman in a long, flowing dress. She has usually developed a bust of unbelievable proportions and the braces are off her teeth. Everyone is struck speechless as a sixty-eight-piece orchestra comes out of the woodwork and she makes her poised entrance.

It's a great scene if you're the mother of a daughter.

But no movie has ever filmed the scene in which a son emerges from the bathroom on prom night wearing white tux and tails, an ascot tie, wing-collar shirt, top hat, gloves, patent leather shoes, and a walking cane and looking like he just fell off a wedding cake.

There are no violins with a son. No magic moment when your eyes meet and there are tears in them. No moment when you throw your arms around him and declare him full-grown. A boy runs around like he has starch in his underwear.

He tries to be cool about the outfit, but you know him well enough to see the anxiety.

Will the toilet tissue clot the blood on his face that he got when he cut himself shaving?

Will his palms sweat when he dances?

Was that spot on the jacket there before he brought it home?

Will the corsage smell like the garlic in the spaghetti next to it in the refrigerator?

Will he have enough money for the restaurant?

Suppose he has to write a check at the restaurant?

Will they cash a check for someone who has no checking account?

Will he end up killing the jerk who talked him into a white satin tux with no pockets?

With a son it's corny to take pictures. Besides, he's late. You have to remember it all. The peck on the cheek. The slam of the door.

You run to the window to watch him climb into a rented limousine that is parked in front of your house and the two houses on either side. It cost more to rent than a week in a cabin at Hawke Lake, but he threatened to self-destruct if he had to appear in public in a station wagon with a bumper sticker that said HAVE YOU HUGGED YOUR CHILDREN TODAY?

You had to rent it for him as he didn't know how to spell "limousine."

The mystique of the boy turned man lasts until you reach the bathroom. Heavy steam settles over fifteen BandAid wrappers, eight wet towels, foam-covered sink, three razor blades, shampoo and soap oozing down the drain, garment bag, boxes, tissue, and a bill for $56.75 impaled on the shower head.

The child lives!

"I need money for a cap and gown to graduate." If you are naïve enough to believe all men and women are created equal, just go to a graduation exercise sometime and look at the graduates all dressed alike.

For a ceremony that is supposed to be universal and dedicated to the principle of conformity, it's a crock. Even in academia, there is no democracy. If you are short, if you have a chest, or if you have a head that is not flat, forget it. Commencement exercises are not for you.

The gowns are basically one-size-fits-all. All of what? All of whom? No one knows. True, the arms are ample. (I only knew of one girl who had to let the sleeves out.) The gowns themselves wrinkle when the lights hit them and hold heat like a silo. The sleeves are designed to weigh down the collar so that halfway through the ceremony it shuts off the air to the windpipe, making breathing impossible.

Graduation gowns were basically made for tall people who weigh no more than 80 pounds. If you are short, you will have to either keep your shoulders lifted or cross your arms over your chest during the entire ceremony.

Speaking of chests, I used to wonder why pleats were a part of the traditional graduation costume. Now I know. Revenge. It's time to punish all the buxom girls who had three dates every Saturday and made their professors forget they were married and had small children. Pleats on a well-endowed girl make her look like she is about to faint backward.

I've done a lot of thinking about mortarboards. I never want to see the man who invented them. I have never seen anyone wear one who was mentally capable of graduating. How they got to the heads of learned men and women is a mystery.

I have seen women jam bobby pins and clips in them, only to have them zing off. Some men have tried putting them on the back or the side of their heads, crushed over their hair.

Millions of people attend graduation ceremonies every year all over the country to pay tribute to those who have attained academic excellence. Underneath that rented mortarboard and gown is a kid in shorts and an obscene T-shirt fighting to get out.

The Ides of May was a force to be dealt with. And just when we thought it was safe to write a check again, she threatened, ''I'm going to college and become a doctor.''

My daughter found me with head bowed over the stack of disposables.

"What are you doing with my graduation gown?"

"The boys cleaned out the closet."

"Those sleaze-buckets," she said. "Why don't they throw out their own stuff? This gown brings back a lot of warm, wonderful memories for me."

My mind raced. She had appreciated all the sacrifice and the love that went into making her moments of high school so special.

"I wore this graduation gown to a Halloween party when I dressed as a pregnant nun with a sign around my neck, THE DEVIL MADE ME DO IT, remember?"

You could die from the sentiment.

"YOU'LL NEVER GUESS WHO THIS IS"

Halloween.

She was four years old. Sitting at the dinner table, her legs dangled like they were hollow. They cleared the floor by a good 20 inches.

She divided her time between chasing a cherry tomato around the plate with a spoon and looking anxiously out of the window pleading, "It's dark already. Isn't it time to go?"

Her costume had been finished for a week. She couldn't wait another minute to put it on.

First came the padding . . . large pillows secured with belts from everyone in the family. Then, large boots to disguise her feet. The baggy pants were next, held up by a rope threaded in the loops and a pair of suspenders.

Charcoal covered the fat cheeks and a bulbous nose looked incongruous on the small face. Large glasses, a large black mustache, and red fright wig completed the outfit.

It was a long drive and a familiar one as she sat on the seat in silence. As we turned the corner, we doused our lights and quietly eased into the driveway to avoid being seen.

"Can you breathe?" I whispered from the bushes.

"Yes," she whispered back.

I pushed the bell and jumped out of sight just as the porch light came on. The door opened and a big voice boomed, "Well, what have we here? It's a beggar, Mother. Do we know any beggars?"

From behind the red fright wig, the slouch hat, and the mustache came a small voice, "You'll never guess who this is, Granddad!"

Of all the holidays on a child's calendar, Halloween seems to be the best—to hold more magic than Christmas, more promise than New Year's, more fun than a birthday, and more pageantry than the Fourth of July. It's supposed to be a prelude to a religious celebration of All Saints' Day, but no one will ever convince me it was not started by a group of mothers who were art majors and seized the opportunity to publicly humiliate the rest of us.

I chose a bad neighborhood from the beginning. The real estate agent tried to warn me. He said, "See that mailbox next door to you? The one with the flowers and butterflies hand-painted? Mrs. Walters did that . . . freehand.''

I thought I could overcome women who shaped their hedges into farm animals, hand-smocked yokes for their daughters' dresses, and made necklaces out of old potato peelings. But it was Halloween that did me in . . . that one day when your children turn to you for your imagination and creativity.

I knew I was in trouble when I saw a hand-carved pumpkin in the window across the street . . . with capped teeth!

The woman on one side of me had been sewing sequins on her daughter's fairy godmother dress since July. The one on the other side was dressing her son as a dragon with a smoke vent on his mask and a bag of dry ice around his neck. It was going to be another year where my kids would stand under a bright porch light with a brown bag over their heads and someone would say, ''What are they, Margaret? Am I missing something?''

My next-door neighbor would never put her cat on her kid's head and tell him to go as Davy Crockett. She would never stick a couple of magazines under his arm and tell him to go as a magazine salesman.

She would never dot her face with lipstick and send her daughter out as a contagious child. (The worst idea I ever had!) She would never spray-paint her son green and tell him he's dressed as a leftover.

As the years went on, picking a costume got tougher and tougher. Everyone dressed so weird and individual to begin with, it was hard to figure out who was "tricking" and who was "treating." My husband still hasn't figured out the difference. He lives in Halloween past when anyone who didn't come to the door in a three-piece suit or a traditional dress was considered "in costume."

Last Halloween the doorbell rang and I heard him exclaim, "Well, what have we here? Silver shoes. A fringed shawl. A comb in the hair. I got it! A Spanish dancer. Come here, Erma, and help me guess who this is."

"For crying out loud," I said, "it's Evelyn picking me up to go to the shopping center."

Minutes later, he ran to the door to discover a bald-headed man with an earring in one ear, a vest, and a tattoo under his right eye.

"A pirate!" he shouted. "How about a nice popcorn ball?"

"How about using the phone?" he grumbled. "My motorcycle broke down and needs a tow."

There was a succession of disappointments, including a woman in moccasins, suede prairie skirt, and a headband, who he thought to be a Native American. (She turned out to be collecting for UNICEF.) And he got real excited about a little kid who had big eyes and was wrinkled who my husband assumed was an extraterrestrial being from another planet. (He was our son's friend who just dropped by after swimming practice and was shriveled.)

I never got over the sadness of his naïveté. "I only gave out one treat," he said, "and that was to a kid who was dressed as a bum. He had a great costume. Faded blue jeans with the knees out, T-shirt cut off above the navel, shoes with holes in them, and a week's growth of beard and a backpack."

Our son is still trying to figure out why his father met him at the door and handed him a popcorn ball.

In retrospect, I don't think there was any part of childhood so hard for my kids to relinquish than Halloween. They wanted it to go on forever. At first I thought it was a matter of how much humiliation they would endure for a crummy pillowcase full of popcorn balls and bubble gum that turned your tongue blue. But it was more than that. It was the last magic kingdom where they could pretend they were someone else. After the land of make-believe came reality, and people who lived there didn't seem to have a whole lot of fun. So they left the night of goblins and witches rather reluctantly.

I noted that each year they took less time to "dress" and went out later. The last year our son went out, he was dressed in a crew-neck sweater and carried a calculator and piece of Brie.

"Give me a hint," I said. "What are you supposed to be?"

"A yuppie," he said.

The kid could have driven to the bank, written his own check, and bought his own candy.

How do you know when you're too old to go begging on Halloween?

How about when the mustache tickles your mask and you can't stand to keep it on?

Or when you can't chew the taffy apples because your partial plate might give way. When someone gives you a kitten and you turn it over and say, "Are you crazy? It isn't even spayed," it's time.

When a sensuous housewife answers the door and asks, "Do I know you?" and you answer, "No, Dollface, but we can fix that," you're too old.

When someone drops a shiny new penny in your bag and you rush right out and drag a Porta Potty to their front porch, you know you've lost the spirit.

When you start "begging" at 11 at night and have to quit at midnight to pick up your date, give it up.

You've graduated to a new plateau . . . when you're a pregnant nun running around in a Volkswagen in search of a party.

"FOR BETTER OR FOR WORSE—BUT NOT FOR LUNCH"

Friday: 9:30 P.M.

I've got a treat for all of you," said my husband. "It just occurred to me, you never saw the slides of your mother and me in the Smokies. Get me a couple more books for the projector. The picture is off the screen. I've got a shot of a dog with one ear standing straight up that will knock your socks off. Last one in, hit the lights."

Reluctantly, the family filed into the darkened room as the slide show began.

"This is one of your mother eating a ham sandwich when she didn't know I was shooting."

From the darkness we heard, "That's disgusting. Put a mirror in front of her."

"You're gonna love this," said their father. "I

103

used my tripod and if you really look close, you can see just the tip of a wing. See it? What kind of bird did we decide that was?''

A flash of light hit the room as a door opened and seconds later, we heard a motor start.

"Here is your mother standing by the state line sign. I like to do that for purposes of identification. Oh, and here's one of your mother and me when we were first married. How did that get in there? Wait a minute.''

There was another flash of light and we heard someone dial a number on the kitchen phone.

"Oh Lord, remember this guy?'' said the narrator. "You kids don't know him. We met him at one of the lakes. Was it Lake Ochichaba? Couldn't get away from the guy. What was his name, Erma? He had a sister in Cleveland. She was a dental assistant. Sounds like Crabtree or . . .''

The door opened and I saw a silhouette of my mother pushing my father out the door.

An hour later my husband said, ''Get the lights and I'll change carousels.''

The audience had thinned out to the two of us.

"That bad,'' he said dejectedly.

"You could throw a war,'' I said, ''and if they knew you were showing home movies, no one would show up.''

"I guess they think we're pretty dull,'' he said.

"Why do you say that?''

"One of them said to me, 'When you're married for thirty-eight years, what do you talk about?' ''

"Show the slide of us as newlyweds again," I said. "I think I'm still wearing the same shoes."

The couple flashed on the screen looking awkward and uncomfortable with the attention.

Had we ever been that young?

I remembered the day so well. As I knelt beside him at the altar, I outlined my plan. First, I was going to talk him into letting his hair grow out. God, I hated that burr. It made him look like a shag rug that had just come out of the dryer. In a couple of months, he wouldn't look like the same man.

At the reception, I watched him with his poker-playing buddies across the room. That would have to change. From here on in, it would be just the two of us watching sunsets and holding hands at the movies.

I'd have to change his eating habits from all those vegetables (designer garbage) to the things that really counted: rolls, pasta, dumplings, and gravy as a beverage.

He was slow and precise. I'd have to come up with a way to speed him up. His personal habits needed work. He never put a cap on a ballpoint pen. He hung up the phone backward because he was left-handed, and his sense of fashion was non-existent. He wore winter clothes in the summer and summer clothes in the winter.

It is thirty-eight years later and absolutely nothing has changed.

My husband stared at the slide, consumed with

his own thoughts. The bride should have marched down the aisle with a Buyer Beware sticker on her forehead. Married a week and she fell apart. Her tonsils became infected, her teeth began to rot, her kidneys became infected, she got three childhood diseases, and she needed glasses. She would have made a great little fixer-upper for some premed student . . . if he had been able to afford her on his salary.

She had an annoying way of dispensing responsibility. She took the appliances as her domain until they broke down and the warranty expired. Then it was always, "You'd better fix YOUR toaster!" The lawn was hers when it came to planting flowers, but when it needed cutting, it was always, "Your lawn is getting ahead of you." There was never any doubt who got custody of the septic tank.

"I wonder if our kids really appreciate the hard work it takes to make a marriage survive," he said, putting on another carousel of slides. "It's a lot of give and take."

I sat in the darkness nodding my head slowly. You don't know give until you're married to a man who controls the television remote tuner, and you don't know take until you sit there through an evening of subliminal experiences of denture creams, breakfast cereals, and wine coolers that all run together.

It was always understood that my husband, Darth Vader, would be the custodian of the television tuner. He regarded the electronic device as his personal "force" of good over evil TV shows. I'm sitting there watching *Dallas*, and just after Sue Ellen says, "Miss Ellie, I've got to sort things out. I thought for a few days I'd go to . . . ," a 90-pound walrus flashes on the screen and Bill Conrad's voice says, ". . . the Bering Sea with thousands of other bulls to mate."

Instinctively, I know he has changed the channel without asking again. I know in my heart that as long as he holds that box in his hand, I will never get back to Southfork.

One night I am comfortably engrossed in a deep, meaningful film when Liv Ullmann suddenly turns into Bea Arthur who turns into Frank Gifford who turns into the Boston Pops who turn into two wrestlers. When I try to explain that Liv is at a crisis in her life and is about to make a major decision about her baby, he says, "I'll turn it back. I just want to see what's on the other channels." By the time he turns Liv back on, the kid has grown up, married, and is talking about his mother in the past tense.

Power. That's what it's all about. Somehow, women just can't capture that same feeling of control by standing on the rubber mat at the supermarket and watching the doors slide back and forth.

"Sometimes," I smiled, "I think our kids think we were born old. It's a shame they didn't know us when we were silly and unpredictable and did dumb things . . . before we became so . . . organized."

My husband was staring at the screen again, lost in his own thoughts.

I married a woman who would bury no garbage before its time! I never saw anything like it. There could be two tablespoons of peas and a pot roast the size of a Kennedy half dollar, and she would say, "Let's save it."

I counted up once. It took an entire week for a leftover to make it to the garbage can.

Day 1: It went from table to refrigerator in an elaborate ritual of joy. "This will make wonderful vegetable soup." Everyone believed her.

Day 2: Every time someone opened the refrigerator door and picked up the leftover, she chanted, "Don't touch it. I'm saving it for vegetable soup."

Day 3: The leftover was moved to a less prominent shelf and occasionally was patted and reassured it had a future in vegetable soup.

Day 4: A traumatic time in the life of future garbage. It was either tossed or was shoved to the rear of the refrigerator on the shelf next to a bowl containing three tablespoons of peach juice and a pit.

Day 5: Traditionally on the fifth day, the leftover was opened, exposed to air, and passed around to see if anyone could identify it. If it was recognizable, it was shoved in a dark corner and allowed to "ripen" for another day. If not, it was history.

Day 6: This was a crucial day in which the peas and beef curdled, turned green, hardened, or grew fuzz.

Day 7: Excited cries resounded through the kitchen as the children danced around the refrigerator chanting, "Is it garbage yet?"

Then Erma would remove the leftovers, fold back the foil, and pronounce the peas and beef dead! Then she would prepare it for burial. First, she wrapped it in newspaper, then put it in a brown bag, then a plastic one, and finally put it to rest in the garbage can in the garage.

I always wanted to put a sign on it, LEFTOVER: BORN MAY 7. DIED MAY 14.

"For what it's worth, Dear, I like your slides," I said, "even though I do feel like a dinosaur."

"Ummm," he said, turning on the light and stacking the carousels. "I read the other day that if a divorce is to occur, it will happen at six and a half years. I wonder what's so mystical about six and a half years."

"It's the marital warranty," I said. "It expires at seventy-eight months."

"What are you talking about?"

"Everything has a level of tolerance. The level of a marriage is six and a half years. At the end of that time, the wife will have cooked 5,408 meals. It's as good or as bad as it's going to get.

"After seventy-eight months, you will have met all the relatives—away from the church. The father-in-law who eats like a Cro-Magnon, the brother who sponges, and the mother-in-law who will call your husband 'the baby' when his gut hangs over his belt buckle and his hairline looks like the state of Florida.''

"You don't know that," he said.

"Trust me. That's the time company manners are put aside, and courtesy is no longer a consideration. Your husband's feet start to smell. His wife leaves toothpaste in the bowl. He cleans his fingernails at the table. She doesn't just blow her nose . . . she flushes it.

"The trousseau is gone. She's down to wearing flannel pajamas and wool socks to bed. There are children to water, feed, educate, clothe, maintain, and discipline. A good-bye kiss in the morning has all the fervor of giving mouth-to-mouth resuscitation to a dead parakeet.''

"My God," he said, "you make it sound like we're serving time.''

"But wait. Occasionally, you see a couple who beats the odds. Did you ever read the section in the newspaper devoted to couples celebrating their fiftieth anniversary? There was one yesterday. Where did you put the paper?''

"Stuffed under the sofa.''

I leafed through until I found it. "Here we go. 'Maudie and Walter Slanker, married fifty years, will be guests of honor at a reception' . . . blah blah . . . listen to this. 'We've hauled water by horse and wagon, coped with the cold and the deep snow, raised and educated a family of ten, and lost a daughter, Virginia.' ''

"She married excitement all right," said my husband.

"Twenty-seven words for a lifetime," I said. "You have to wonder. Were there other moments? Did they hang wallpaper together? Argue about who slept next to the wall? Toast no-baby month? Become jealous of an encyclopedia salesman?

"Did she get sick of his same jokes year after year? Did he tire of hearing about her arthritis? Did they wonder about their future together the year he taught her how to drive? The year his mother baby-sat and cleaned her oven? Was he cheap? Was she boring?

"Did he have an annoying habit of picking his teeth with his tongue and making a clicking noise that drove her up the wall? Did she say every night for thirty years when he walked through the front door, 'Is that you?'

"Did they really love one another through fevers, flu, fatness, nausea, irritability, and sarcasm—or did they just hang on?

"Were they there for one another when Virginia died, when he lost his job, or when she felt neglected?

"Did he ever know she hated peppers in the meat loaf but for fifty years put them in because he liked them? Did he ever suspect she hated house slippers without heels but wore the ones he bought every Christmas?

"Ten children . . . that's a lot of shoes, a life-time of overbites, an eternity of 'Can I's' . . . endless evenings of PTA, years of slammed doors, and an uninterrupted span of 'We've got the children to think about.' ''

I put my head on my husband's shoulder. ''Fifty years. How did they do it?''

My husband sighed, ''He probably had hopes of getting in the last word.''

A CHILD'S BATHROOM
IS HIS CASTLE

Friday: 11 P.M.

As my husband packed away the projector, I noted the calm that had once again come over the house, with all three of the kids out pursuing whatever it was they pursued at 11 o'clock at night.

"I think I'll go up and check the 'guest rooms.' "

"Since when did the kids' bedrooms get to be guest rooms?" asked my husband.

"Don't start. I told you before, I like the idea of a room making a statement. The bedrooms say, 'Don't settle in. Your visit is only temporary.' "

"The minute they moved out, everything around here changed," he said. "You put a tablecloth on our kitchen table, and the next thing you know, it

113

was a 'breakfast room.' And a lamp and a chair turned our bedroom into a 'suite.' I'll never understand why you took the pool table out of the family room.''

"Because we no longer had a family," I said patiently. "Besides, the pool table looks better in the sun room."

"It got the same amount of sun when it was just the back porch," he grumbled. "Besides, I miss the desk in the—what is it you call it now?"

"The 'media room.' "

"I don't see why you had to put it in with your sewing machine."

"Maybe you'd like it better in your workshop?"

"Where is my workshop?" he asked.

"You know very well it's in the old basement with your tools."

"What tools?" he said. "I got a hammer, a screwdriver, a dozen baby food jars with screws stored in them, and two broken-down lawn chairs. All I want is a nice room where I can sit down and read a paper in some kind of privacy. I can't even go to the bathroom to be alone anymore."

"That's because we don't have a bathroom. Since we put the exercise bicycle and the bathroom scale in there, it's a 'personal fitness' room."

He smiled, "Have you seen your personal fitness room since the kids came home?"

I kicked open the door to the personal fitness room and gasped. The mirror was fogged with steam, towels were strewn wall to wall, the shower curtain dripped water on the floor, soap turned from a solid state to a liquid before my eyes, tubes without caps dotted the sink. The toilet tissue spindle was empty. Wet washcloths and dirty clothes hung from the exercise bicycle. Newspapers littered the floor. The toilet was filled with Band-Aid wrappers. Opened bottles of shampoo and rinses lined the bathtub, and a hair dryer was left in the bowl.

It should have been called the "children's playroom." Ever since I could remember, it was their social watering hole. They came in here at the age of two, and barring major holidays and occasional stabs at education, we didn't see them again until it was time for them to get their own apartments.

What did they do in there? They projected home movies of Mommy and Daddy into the toilet bowl and then flushed so our faces would swirl and appear distorted.

They floated light bulbs in the bathtub and shot at them with water pistols. They wrapped a dead horned toad in a flag once and buried him at "sea." They decorated the toilet seat like a cake, using Dad's shaving cream for the lettering.

And when I pounded on the door and shouted, "What are you doing in there?" the response was always the same. "Nothing."

"Nothing" translates into something quite different for a parent and a child.

"Nothing" to a parent means you are staring

into space with your hands in your lap, your eyes glazed, and your breathing shallow.

When a child is doing "nothing," that is a signal for parents to dial 911. He is usually doing "nothing" behind a closed bathroom door, a dog is barking, water is running under the door, a sibling is begging for mercy, and there is a strange odor of burning fur and the sound of a thousand camels running in place.

I always wanted to know how long they had been doing "nothing," whom they were doing "nothing" with, and how come it took them fifteen minutes to answer the question.

Kids are drawn to a bathroom like a magnet. There's a mystique about it from birth. Immediately after they enter the world, an inner voice says, "As soon as you learn how to walk or crawl, Bippie, you can toddle into the bathroom and throw your shoes into the toilet."

"What are shoes?" asks the infant.

"Something you take off your feet every chance you get."

"What's a toilet?"

"The place you throw your shoes in to make it bubble."

I looked around. I had spent the best years of my life in this dreary steam bath trying to train one of them to a toilet seat. I wish I had a dime for every day I put a kid on the throne and sat on the edge of the bathtub and described the water scenes from *Deliverance*. Sometimes I threatened them with a hole in their bicycle seat and a plastic liner in their tux at the prom.

They spent so much time in the bathroom, they thought the sky had a light and an exhaust fan in it. Small wonder they grew up with an affinity for this room. It became their retreat . . . their mountaintop . . . their last bastion of privacy. It assured them diplomatic immunity from every chore you can think of.

"Where's your brother? I want him to help carry in the groceries from the car."

"He's in the bathroom."

"Hurry up or you're going to miss your school bus and I'll have to drive you to school."

"I'm in the bathroom."

"Are you in bed?"

"I'm in the bathroom."

"Could you let the dog out?"

"I'm in the bathroom."

"Come to dinner!"

"I'm in the bathroom."

In my nightmares, I could hear a minister at the altar saying to the bride, "Where is the bridegroom?" and a voice from the distance shouting, "I'm in the bathroom."

Looking back, I realized most of my communication with the kids was exchanged outside of this very door, usually at 2 in the morning.

"Are you home?"

"Who did you think it was?"

"What time is it?"

"What time do you think it is?"

"Have you eaten?"

"Don't I always?"

"Did Greg get in touch with you?"

"Did he call?"

"Did you get gas for the car?"

"Didn't I say I would?"

"Are there any towels in there?"

"Aren't there always?"

"Do you want me to call you late in the morning?"

"Are you serious?"

"I'm going to bed. It's wonderful that we can talk together like this. A lot of kids when they reach your age become uncommunicative and you don't know what they're doing or thinking. Am I lucky or what? Don't answer that!"

As I wiped the last of the water off the floor, I stood up and surveyed the room with pride.

"The personal fitness room once more meets health standards," I announced proudly.

"It will always be the library to me," said my husband, as he entered with a stack of newspapers.

"Before you get settled," I said, "I want the bathroom scale."

"Where are you going with it?" he asked.

"To the 'reptile room.' Another twenty pounds on top of the snake cage can't hurt."

"BUT DAD . . .
IT'S A CLASSIC!"

Saturday: 8 A.M.

Watching them from the window, they looked like a scene from *Father Knows Best*. Dad in his coat sweater circled his son's car, stopping occasionally to kick the tires and huddle over the motor. His son, slightly taller than his father, in raggy jeans and tousled hair, waved a wrench in his hand.

Was it only a few years ago the father had black hair and the son wore bathing trunks the size of a coaster and they were standing together in that same spot to dedicate the swimming pool?

Kids we had never seen before were lined up with snorkels, rubber ducks, rafts, and old inner tubes from semi trucks.

"For God's sake," said his father, "I don't even

119

have the thing inflated yet. Didn't you tell them it's plastic, it's only 48 inches in diameter and 14 inches deep? I've ordered bigger drinks!''

As he put his lips to the valve, a hush fell over the crowd. After ten minutes of gasping and blowing, he was ready to pass out, but the pool was inflated. As he stood over the plastic pool with a garden hose, the group's eyes were riveted to the trickle of water. He held the crowd back while he added bleach and swished it around. When he finished he said, "Now, we're going to lay a few ground rules. No jumping in with grass on your feet and . . ." He and his words were drowned . . . literally. Two seconds later a neighbor child appeared at the door and announced our son had gone to the bathroom in the pool and they were all going home.

They may have had their differences in the past, but today they were . . . communicating.

The door slammed shut with a fury that jarred the dishes. "Didn't I tell you buying that pile of junk was a mistake!''

"But Dad, it's a classic.''

"You can't tell him anything," said my husband, addressing his remarks to me.

"What's the matter?" I asked.

"The matter is," said my husband, "that that car was a lemon from the word go. Did you ever wonder who buys all those cars driven on television on *The Rockford Files* or *The Dukes of Hazzard?* Our kids buy 'em.''

"Dad, the car was a '79 and only had 500 miles on it."

"That's because it was a getaway car."

"Hatchbacks are classics."

"It wasn't a hatchback until a garage door fell on it, haven't you figured that out? The tailpipe is held on with electrician's tape, the windows are stationary, the springs are shot, and the motor won't turn over."

"In ten years," said my son pointing his finger, "that little baby will be worth its weight in gold."

"It's going to take you ten years to get a transmission for it that's available only in a small town in Czechoslovakia! You better get your act together, Mister, that car is going to take money . . . lots of it."

"I take care of the car," he said defensively.

"Pouring Orange Crush in the radiator when it boils over is not taking care of it."

"If it's such a bummer, how come someone tried to steal it last month?"

"If it's such a gem, how come they caught them trying to hot-wire it to get it started when the key was in the ignition?"

"I didn't ask for a lecture. All I'm asking for is a lousy $200 to get it running again."

"Look, Son," said his father, "ever since you graduated from college you've been trying to find yourself. You wanta know where you are? You're somewhere between Clearasil and bankruptcy. I have a dream for you, Son. I want to see you join hands with a steady job at the altar of employment and promise to love and to cherish from this day forward, for retirement benefits or for mergers . . . for pay raises or layoffs . . . in slumps and stock splits . . . till death do you part. You need an incentive? For better or for worse, you're married to a 'classic' sitting in the side yard with bucket seats and a name you can't pronounce. You're committed to it in sickness and in health for as long as you can afford gas, insurance, license fees, and tune-ups. You have responsibilities now. You have a car to support! Get a job!''

Our son listened carefully and headed for the guest room.

For a first-generation speech, I had to admit it was pretty good. Usually, our lectures were Golden Oldies handed down from our parents, which their parents had laid on them. But this was a new speech for a new generation living in new times. No one had to tell our generation how to find the American Dream. The molds were in place when we got there. We married early, had babies, wore practical polyester, paid cash, fertilized grass, washed our own cars, and waited for the Christmas savings check. We accepted twenty-year house payments, forty-year marriages, and thirty years on the same job without question.

It wasn't until we had children that we discovered no one wanted to emulate us or our life-style. No one wanted to inherit the fruits of our labor. No one wanted to profit from our experiences.

They had their own timetable.

Our generation brought with us the curse of memory. We remembered when jobs were nonexistent and there was only one way out of a world of sleeping in your underwear and buying coal fifty cents at a time . . . an education!

I don't think we could ever forget the feeling of pride of watching our first college graduate weave down the aisle.

He looked like a Supreme Court judge who had just shot a few baskets and had forgotten to change his shoes.

I snapped a picture, even though he had threatened to self-destruct if I did it. I looked. He was still there looking at me like he had eaten something that didn't agree with him.

His father and I had disagreed on his choice of university. I thought the campus had a nice "feeling" to it—much like *The Paper Chase* on PBS. I never lost my naïveté. When my son didn't write home, I knew it was because he dropped a bible on his foot and couldn't hobble to the post office to mail his letter.

When he intercepted his grades before we could open them, I knew in my heart he wanted to have them framed and given to me for Mother's Day.

As I told his father, I know he postdated a check for $100 so he could buy a jacket to go with his tie for the one evening a week they dressed for dinner at the dorm.

Even when we phoned him at the dorm and a

voice shouted, "Suds! It's your Mom!" there was no doubt in my mind I had dialed the wrong number.

My husband took one look at the curtains flapping outside the dormitory windows, a three-story monument to beer cans near the chapel, and a goat tethered in the student lounge, and said, "You are wrong. It's *Animal House*."

Had it only been four years since he sat at our dining room table and worked out his curriculum? At first I thought the subjects were frivolous, until our son explained there was a movement underfoot to make college students more literate.

"What will they think of next?" I smiled.

"The general consensus," he added, "is that advanced education has swung too far toward specialized studies and needs to get back to courses that prepare students for life."

I couldn't agree more.

He had done well in "Remedial Bicycle Watching" (three hours) designed for the novice who has had three bicycles ripped off in five years. "Bring chains, locks, small explosives, and detonator. Bicycles will be furnished."

"Is There Life After Lunch?" was enlightening (three hours). "A seminar with guest lecturers who outline advantages of staying awake to participate in cleaning room, soaking laundry, doing required reading, and, in the final quarter, adding a class or two."

He barely squeaked through "Your Car and Faith

Healers'' (two hours). This was "a frank look at automobile mechanics who promise to fix your transmission by adding water." As a bonus, Dr. Weingard Schuyler, Heart Institute, conducted a lecture on how to survive an insurance premium notice after a claim has been filed.

No one will know how he crammed for "Parent Weekend: Religious Experience or End of the World as You Know It." This covered all aspects of getting it together before your parents appeared on campus, including how to make a roommate of the opposite sex disappear and how to decorate your room with academic accessories like books and pencils. Guaranteed to give new meaning to "have a good day."

The course he felt did him the most good was "Jogging For Bodies," a five-hour fun approach to physical fitness in which warm-ups were eliminated and the emphasis was on meeting members of the opposite sex.

I thought he chose his courses of study rather wisely, but my husband said he feared that a general education would promote intellectual conformity and a sterile acquiescence for the sake of social cohesion. I told him, "The boy *wanted* to take 'Social Cohesion' the last semester, but he needed the 'History of Perrier' to graduate."

To appease his father, he actually took a job-related course called "Cinema." He always loved going to the movies. At first we thought it would be fun to have a child who could splice together some of our home movie shots of South America. That was until we discovered he edited the shortest home movie ever recorded in the *Guinness Book of World Records*. As he explained to us, ''There was only ten feet of film that had any quality to it whatsoever. I cannot believe you left home without a dolly for the camera.''

Our son, the college graduate. He was so naïve when we sent him off to this school. We tried to give him insights that would help him in his first living experience away from the family . . . insights that would help him guide his life through troubled waters:

Clean underwear does not reproduce itself.

Classmates who owe you money drop out of school in their freshman year to get in touch with their feelings at Big Sur.

Students who write their parents get remembered in the will.

Deposits should at all times exceed withdrawals.

Pursue every roach as if it were female, pregnant, and crazy to come home with you in your luggage.

A note from the library, telling your parents that unless you return the volume of *Erotic Dreams and What They Mean* to the library you will receive a blank diploma, will throw your mother into cardiac arrest.

And now it had all come together. They called his name and before he left the stage he checked to make sure the diploma was not blank.

The commencement speaker said the graduates were the hope of the future. He said each of them would create new horizons and focus on their destiny. The band played softly from *The Sound of Music* in the background and eyes misted as the speaker challenged them to "Climb every mountain, ford every stream, follow every highway till you find your dream."

The kid couldn't find his car after graduation.

Our son returned to the kitchen and said, "Dad, I've been thinking about what you said and you're right. I've really screwed up and I'm going to do something about it. I'm going back to college for my masters."

Both of us sat lifeless, our coffee cups frozen in midair. I had given birth to a marathon student. He would be just like Harv Stidwell, a guy I knew in the class of '47, '48, '49, '50, '51, '52, and '53 who was a baton twirler. He had more than 1,500 friendship pictures and was the only student who knew all the words to the school song. Someone said he went right from the GI Bill to Medicare before he graduated one summer with fifteen majors and twenty-three minors.

"And I've even solved the car problem," said our son. "I'll move back home and borrow yours."

"MOM AND DAD!
I'M HOME!"

It wasn't fair.

I already said good-bye to The Grateful Dead and Chicago. Good-bye to empty milk cartons and dried-out lunch meat.

I said so long forever to porch lights that burned all day and night for three years and to mildewed towels and empty ice cube trays. I'm too tired for my old profession—mothering. You have to be in condition to do that . . . like an athlete. I no longer care that my dish towels look like the seat of a mechanic's pants or that my cookie sheet was born the same year as Alan Alda.

No longer can I leap into the air in glorious exhilaration when my laundry smells fresh or glide my hands across a bathtub that doesn't feel gritty.

There was a time when I knew exactly when a kid was going to split and get out of taking out the garbage. They move too fast for me now.

Face it, the body is gone. Legs that used to run trays up to the bedroom eighteen times a day for a common cold have more ridges than corduroy. The form that used to drag out every morning and feed everyone now burrows under the cover like a lump and whimpers.

I'm not ready to open up the kitchen again for three-a-day and a matinee on Saturdays. With just the two of us, the kitchen became a place where we went for a drink of water. To some, a $20,000 drinking fountain might be considered excessive, but we earned it.

We "dine" out now. I wait until the waiter is near the table and drop the name of Mikhail Baryshnikov because I like to pronounce it. My husband sniffs a wine cork and blesses it. We talk about El Salvador. I don't know how long it will last, but right now it's fun being phonies.

It has nothing to do with loving my children. I also have affection for Miss Piggy, but I don't want to turn her underwear right side out before I have to launder them.

It's not fair. The kids come home when they're out of work, out of money, out of socks, out of food, and in debt.

They're never here when they're in love, in the bucks, in transit, in school, and their cars are running.

Well, it's going to be different this time. There will have to be rules.

Anything that dies in the room must be buried before the sun sets on it.

In the event of missing towels, glassware, food, and silverware, a parent has the right to search and seizure.

Parents have the right to break down the door when it is too quiet.

Boxes and luggage used for the return from an apartment/trip/marriage will be left in the garage for thirty days of deroaching before being allowed in the house.

No stereo system will be permitted on the premises without headphones.

Parents are not only allowed to accept payment for their room, but also will insist upon it.

People left in the room longer than sixty days must have a forwarding address.

I honestly don't think it's going to work. Even on short visits, we fall short. Our kids say we support the wrong causes on our bumper stickers. We do not take the world seriously enough. We watch mindless television, and our friends perpetuate foreign imports.

We dress too young. We think too old. We eat too fast. We drive too slow. Our car is too big. Our closets are too small.

Oh God, our closets. There go our closets!

I'll have to revert again to hiding anything of

value or having them sift through my things like a discount house on Saturday night.

Oh, I used to be giving, loving, and sharing. But that was before I realized a woman who is giving, loving, and sharing ends up with a drawer full of dirty panty hose, a broken stereo, and a wet toothbrush every morning.

Also, a camera with sand in it, a blouse that died from acute perspiration, a library book with a bent back, a sleeping bag with a broken zipper, a tennis racket with a cracked frame, and a transistor that "just went dead when it hit the pavement."

I'm a mother. Somewhere it is written that when children have something to spit out, we extend our hands. On the same tablet, it is recorded that sheets that have to be washed in the middle of the night are women's work. It came with the territory. But where does it say I have to loan my car to my kids?

My car is a clean car. A clean car is a happy car. It isn't used to life in the fast lane. It's never been to a rock concert in the middle of a cornfield or a dirt bike race along some dusty road. It hasn't been out past midnight since I owned it and it exudes innocence. It's a lady.

My son borrowed it once . . . a night I'm not likely to forget. I was awake when the car spun into the driveway with music so loud my teeth cramped, and I had only to look at it the next morning to see the mud on her grill and the seat belt flapping beneath the door to know that my car had been *violated*! She had that "used" and "empty" look about her.

Her motor had been raced. She had blown a speaker. All the push buttons on the radio had been repunched to rock stations. There was a piece of cold pizza in her ashtray. Her antenna was high enough to clear the Rockies. There was a tennis ball lodged under her accelerator.

She looked like she hadn't cooled off in a week. Her gas gauge was on E.

That has always been one of the mysteries of life . . . how kids can run a tank of gas right down to the last thimbleful.

It's a gift, really. The car will roll into the driveway, gasp, thrust forward, die, and the gas gauge will drop like a stone to E.

One time I even took one of the kids in the car with me and said, "Do you know where Mother is taking you? We're going to a place where you have never been before."

"Will there be kids there my own age?" he asked.

"Not many, but mingle and make friends."

As we pulled in front of the pumps, he said, "What is this place?"

"It's a gas station. You take a nozzle from the pump, put it into the gas tank, and the fuel converts to energy and makes the car run."

"Are you serious?" he asked.

"Surely," I said, "you have had some curiosity

as to why they put out signs on these that say LAST STOP UNTIL FREEWAY?''

"I thought they were rest rooms," he said.

All over America, wherever teenagers gather, the subject comes up. "Where were you and what were you doing when you found out about a gas pump?"

I looked out the window as the prodigal son poked under the hood of his car. He, too, would have some adjusting. He would return home as a man and be treated as a child once more. His independence would be compromised by, "Where are you going? and "What time are you getting home?" I remembered when he was a toddler. We had gone to the grocery store and, ignoring my threats, he reached up and pulled over a bubble gum machine that broke and sent colored balls of gum all over the store. He was terrified as I lashed out at him angrily, "That does it, Buster! You will never see another Oreo cookie for as long as you live."

Tears welled in his eyes as he desperately searched the faces in the crowd for some sign of compassion. Finally, he threw his arms around my knees for comfort. I, who a moment ago had rejected him.

Why me? I was all he had, and he knew beneath the anger the love was always there.

MOMMIE AND DADDIE DEAREST!

Saturday: 9:15 A.M.

"Hey, look who's up!" said one of the boys. "Our sister! What's the matter, did your mattress catch fire?"

"Where's the coffee?"

"If you want a Danish . . . they're history."

"I do not want a Danish. I do not eat breakfast," she said tiredly.

"Remember what Mom used to tell you? There was a buzzard following you all the way to the bus stop."

"Please. What kind of disgusting cereal is that?"

"Fibre-Bran Nuggets. It's caffeine-free, no sugar, no preservatives, and makes its own gravy.

134

Box tops will earn you premiums on African violets and a whoopie cushion for your hemorrhoids."

"God you're gross!" said his sister. "It looks like Dad is still putting all the old stale cereal into one box like no one notices."

"Remember the time he combined Chock Full of Pimples with Puffed Crunchees and Cavity Flakes? The milk turned purple."

"Oh, and remember the cereal embargo. No cereal was to be brought into the house until every cereal on the shelf was eaten. There was an outbreak of cereal incest and we ended up with eight boxes more than we started."

"Where are Mom and Dad?" asked our daughter.

"Jogging."

"But the car is gone."

"You don't think they walk to the jogging path?"

"Are they a pair to draw to . . . or what?"

"Frankly," said a son, "I think we're too old to sit for a Christmas card picture."

"So, what's wrong with that? Besides, Mom and Dad like having us home. Makes them feel young and needed again."

"Did you see her last night? She poured me half a glass of milk and told me not to spill it. The woman still doesn't trust me."

"Why should she?" said his brother. "Your whole life's been a lie beginning with the time you stuffed all your papers down the sewer so you wouldn't be late for a Little League game."

"You should talk," he charged. "You were supposed to bring Mom to school when you were caught belching the 'Ave Maria' during Mass and you told the school she was out of town."

"Hey, what could I do?" he retaliated. "I was thinking of becoming a priest and I didn't want it on my record."

"If they only knew half of the things we did when we were kids, they wouldn't have permitted us to grow up," said his sister.

"They weren't perfect either," said our son. "Mom used to put us outside to play when the chill factor was 70° below zero. She said, 'Get a little fresh air. It's good for you.' "

"And I know for a fact she gave us tranquilizers on our vacation and told us they were vitamins."

"No wonder when I crayoned I couldn't keep within the lines."

"Yeah, but you all got the young parents," said the baby of the group. "Since you guys screwed up, she came down hard on me so they wouldn't make the same mistake and get the same results. Like how old did she tell you she was before she was allowed to drive a car?"

The oldest said, "She told me she was twenty-one."

The middle child said, "She told me twenty-four."

The baby said, "She wanted me to vulcanize my feet."

"Are we talking about the same Mom? The thin,

bright-eyed dark-haired girl who used to read me stories, bake cookies, paste my baby pictures in the album, and giggle a lot?''

The middle child said, ''The somber-looking bleached blonde who used to put me to bed at 6:30 and bought me a dog to save on napkins?''

The baby said, ''The grayish lady who falls asleep during the 6 o'clock news and is going to show me my baby pictures when she takes the rest of the roll at my wedding?''

''That's another thing. They go to bed right after the 10 o'clock news. Do you suppose they're all right?''

''Their social life is somewhere to the right of a sedated parakeet.''

''You know Dad. He hates surprises. They were going out one night and I heard him ask Mom, 'Am I going to have a good time? Who is going to be there? Will I stay awake? What time are we coming home?' ''

''We were sitting there the other night watching television and the phone rang and do you know what he said? He said, 'Who could that be at this hour?' It was 8:30!''

They thought about it awhile before one son spoke. ''Did you ever wonder why Mom got married?''

''That's easy. She needed a personal slave . . . someone to answer the phone, get her sweater, find her glasses, and move the garden hose every five minutes.''

"I thought it was to have someone to eat the leftovers that the dog wouldn't touch."

"I always thought she was doing research and was going to establish the first New York Sock Exchange."

"Oh Lord. The wash-and-spin Bermuda Triangle. I hadn't thought about that in years. She was rather crazed in the utility room. I thought for awhile she was losing it."

"Queen of the Static Cling. I can see her now on her hands and knees rummaging around the dryer and mumbling, 'If a pair of socks went in . . . then a pair of socks must come out.' "

"Remember Dad? He came home once with a dozen pairs of new socks, tore them apart, and threw out one sock from each pair to save her the trouble of losing them."

"I asked her where my other sock went once and she said, 'It went to live with Jesus.' Parents have an answer for everything."

"Yeah, every time Mom said, 'I'm doing this because I love you,' I knew it was going to be something rotten. Where do they get those phrases?"

"You mean like, 'This is going to hurt me worse than it does you'?"

"You know what I think?" said the older son. "I think there's a book of them that the hospital passes out on the day they take the baby home from the hospital, *Wise Sayings for Parents*."

"I remember Mom telling me, 'When you grow

up you'll thank me for being so strict.' I'm grown up and I'm still ticked off about it."

"Or how about when Dad says, 'Son, I may not always understand you, but I'm willing to listen.' He says that just before he says, 'I don't want to hear anymore. Go to your room.' "

"And if there's anyone in this room who can spread world-class guilt like Mom with that one little phrase . . ."

All three of them chanted in unison, "Never mind! I'll do it myself."

"God, I hated that!" said a son. "I could be watching the last five seconds of a Super Bowl game, with the score even and my team is kicking a field goal, and Mom says, 'Can you get this lid off the pickles for me?' and one-half second later she says, 'Never mind, I'll do it myself.' "

"Is that the time she used a meat cleaver and a rolling pin to open it and her hand required six stitches?"

"Jesus, that woman can make St. Joan of Arc, Mother Theresa, and a thousand women suffering in labor look like terrorists."

"Hey, aren't we coming down a little hard on them?" asked their sister. "Can you honestly sit there and say you have no regrets about some of the things you've pulled off?"

"Here it comes . . . the old killing my goldfish by dropping it behind the dresser and saying nothing while Mom paid $50 for the exterminator because something smelled bad story."

"That's pretty good for starters," she said. "How about the time you left the gas grill on all night on the back porch and we didn't have a back porch the next morning?"

"I thought surely they would put me in an institution for that trick," said the youngest.

"I think Mom aged fifteen years the time you jumped off the roof with her dish towel around your neck saying you were Superman."

"Get a load of Snow White," said one of the boys. "I seem to remember our sister requiring stitches on her lip from kissing a boy with braces and telling Mom she fell into the locker."

"Both of them have a scary quality for knowing what you do when they don't see it or hearing what you mean when you don't say it."

"You know," said a son, "you spend a lifetime trying to please them and just when you think you're what they want you to be, they'll pull the string and nearly choke you to death, but all in all they're O.K."

"Speaking of being asphyxiated, did I tell you I'm moving back home?" said our son.

"That oughta make Mom's Christmas. Knowing her, she's ecstatic," said our daughter. "She's the original earth mother."

"I think both of 'em were pretty knocked out. Neither of them could speak."

"It's not such a bad idea. They need someone to keep an eye on 'em. Have you noticed, it takes two of them to finish a sentence anymore."

"That's nothing new. Mom's always been a little flaky. Remember when we were growing up? There were only three of us and she could never remember which one she was talking to. She'd go through all the names before she stumbled on the right one."

"Yeah," said a son. "Once I wore my PJs wrong-side-out and she called me Dr. Denton for a week."

"She used to say to me, 'How long do I have to call you before you answer?' and I'd say, 'Until you get it right.' Then when she got the name right, she couldn't remember what she called me for."

"I read somewhere that every day after the age of thirty-five you lose 100,000 brain cells."

"What's that supposed to mean?"

"It means every day of their lives, the pilot light gets dimmer, the elevator goes to fewer floors, it takes longer for the pot to boil."

"God, that's heavy."

"After awhile, it will take two of them to work a parking meter."

"They'll probably call one of us up to come over and set the FM station on their car radio."

"We may even find them passed out one day on the kitchen floor from an overdose of bran."

"It's sorta sad. They used to be such vibrant, active people."

"Hey, it happens. You're born. You live, and one day the wavy line on the terminal by your bed gets a hum in it and fades to black."

There was a long silence. Finally, our daughter said, ''Look at it this way. Mom and Dad have led long, productive lives.''

''Yeah,'' her brother added, ''and someday we'll be in our forties.''

THE FAMILY THAT
PLAYS TOGETHER . . .
SHOULDN'T

I threw my body in the $45 hot pink warm-up suit against a tree to stretch the hamstrings that were supported by $80 jogging shoes. Taking off the $12 orange sweatband, I wiped the designer sweat off my face and groaned.

A breathless husband joined me.

"How did you beat me back?" he panted. "I didn't see you on the path. The last time I passed you, you were tying your shoe."

It was a trick he never caught on to. Every day for four months I started out with him on the jogging path, ran fifty yards, and stopped to retie my shoe. Then I just dawdled and talked.

It made all the difference in my life. When people discovered I "ran," they began to tell me how healthy I looked and how much weight I had lost.

Perfect strangers would come up to me and ask if I was going to run a 10K Sunday. Besides, it did a lot for my hormonal balance to hear heavy breathing behind me. You can't buy that kind of excitement over the counter.

I sat on the ground and watched my husband perform the cool-down ritual.

"I thought maybe the kids would join us this morning," he said.

"Are you crazy? Our daughter thinks cellulite is a battery, and the closest your sons ever got to an accelerated heartbeat is when you told them they had to take the bus to school instead of the car."

"C'mon," he said, "you act like they're a bunch of couch potatoes. They were always into athletics in high school, remember?"

How could I ever forget those athletic banquets where I sat there hearing about sons I had never known before? Who were these enigmas who were comatose at home and came to life on a school campus?

I sat there stunned one night as the coach put his arm around our son's neck and announced to a crowd, "This boy is probably one of the best sprinters I've had in my entire career here at South High. Hang onto your hats, folks. He set a school record this year by running the 100-yard dash in 9.9!"

Everyone clapped and rose to their feet.

9.9! I figured it had to be nine days and nine hours. I once asked him to run the garbage out to the can and it sat by the sink until it turned into a bookend.

And in a testimonial to another son, a coach said, "I don't know what this baseball team would have done without this boy's hustle. We've had chatterers on the team before who get the boys whipped up, but this one is a world-class chatterer. There isn't a moment when he isn't saying something to spark the team when they're down."

Our son smiled boyishly and hung his head.

Chatterer? From a kid who spoke only six words to me a week: When you going to the store?

I must have sat through a dozen of these banquets listening to coaches present a courtesy award to our kid who displayed sportsmanship and manners on the tennis court. By pure coincidence, it was the same boy who broke his brother's face the day before for "stealing" a record album from his room.

I was numbed by the announcement that one of our children threw a ball weighing eight pounds a distance of 100 feet. He couldn't throw a six-ounce Saturday edition of the newspaper from his bike to a porch on his paper route.

"Have you forgotten how your son got an award for picking up wet towels and suits for an entire swim team and couldn't pick up his own feet at home?" I asked.

"You know how kids are," he said. "They're

two personalities. One for home and one for show. We're blessed. You and I share the same interests, the same values, the same respect for one another. That's why we're such a good team. We work well together and we play well together. Even when we play Trivial Pursuit.''

Give me a break! You show me a woman who plays Trivial Pursuit with her husband and I'll show you a woman in a singles' bar.

My husband had a smirk on his face from the minute he threw the dice and read the question, ''How many stars are in Orion's belt?''

The entire family huddled over the Trivial Pursuit board, snickered, and nudged one another.

''She doesn't know that,'' said my father. ''Give me the dice.''

''How do you know I don't know that!'' I snapped.

''Mom,'' said my son, ''anyone who doesn't know what candy bar is made in Hershey, Pennsylvania, cannot possibly know how many stars are in Orion's belt.''

''You didn't say that to your grandmother when you asked her what the biggest gland in the body was.''

''I knew it was the liver,'' said Mother.

''She guessed,'' I charged.

''She did not,'' said Dad, ''she just remembered her brother.''

''That's a pretty crummy thing to say,'' said Grandma.

"Give Mom a break," said my daughter. "Science and literature questions are hard!"

"She couldn't even remember that Barbara Billingsley was the Beav's mother," said a son.

"Why should she remember that?" asked my dad.

"Because they both wear a girdle when they clean the oven," said my husband.

"Time is up," said my son.

"My God," I said, "I've raised a child who would turn me in to the Nazis if I had a radio in World War II."

"Do you know the answer or not?"

"She'd know how many stars in Joan Collins' belt," said my husband.

The dice moved on.

Was it my imagination, or was I developing a nun wish? Sometimes my husband could be the kindest man in the world. Other times, he made me feel like I was lobotomized by domesticity. I'll never forget him on that trip to Spain a few years back. We were sitting there on the beach like Roy Rogers and Dale Evans. He was fishing; I was needlepointing. When we heard someone crawling over the rocks, we both turned. A bather—totally nude—was making her way toward the water. For a full five minutes, my husband and I turned to statues of salt.

She walked toward the water, searching the shoreline for rocks. At one point my husband cleared his throat and I thought he was going to say something, but he didn't.

Finally, she entered the water and swam out to a rock about fifty feet away and stretched out to catch some rays.

My husband turned to me and said, "Did you see that? She wasn't wearing shoes. She could have cut her feet to ribbons on these rocks."

"You really are certifiable, aren't you? Here's a tramp who invades our space, and the only thing you see are her tender feet."

"How do you know she's a tramp?" he asked. "She looks like she has a nice personality."

"She has the intelligence of a food processor."

"You don't know that either," he snapped.

"When you leave an ankle bracelet on in salt water, you're not too bright."

"Well, she obviously comes from a good family. Possibly military."

"How can you possibly arrive at a revelation like that?"

"Her posture," he said. "It's superb."

"I cannot believe how naïve you are. Would you want your son to marry someone with a tattoo of a duck on her hip?"

"It was not a duck. It was a family crest of some kind."

"Right. And Prince Charles has two lions tattooed on his bicep. Why are you so stubborn about this Woodstock dropout?"

"And why are you so vindictive and judgmental

about a person you haven't seen . . . fully clothed. Frankly, I'd like to see her in our family.''

"She comes into this family and I go out," I said, jamming my needlepoint in the bag.

"Is this an ultimatum?"

"You bet your sweet bird it is. I hope you and your Dr. Ruth out there will be very happy.''

At this point, a male nude bather, wearing only a wedding ring, jumped into the water and joined our nymph friend on the rock.

"Now, *he's* slime," said my husband.

"I don't know," I said, "he strikes me as someone who would be very nice to his mother.''

My attention came back to the game in progress.

My dad was admonishing my mother for remembering that Miss America played "Nola" on her nose to win the talent competition in 1953 but never remembering to put starch in his shirts.

My husband accused his son of remembering that Wilt Chamberlain made 23,924 rebounds in his career but never remembering to put oil in his car.

My daughter said if her brother didn't take his turn so she could make a phone call, she was going to rearrange his face, and Mother was in a trance trying to remember who played the part of Melanie's baby in *Gone With the Wind*.

I realized a family has no allies. There are no pacts based on honor or loyalty between any of its members. Your confidante could sing like a canary. Your loyal booster could abandon you and turn into an adversary. The man who held your hand tenderly through sixteen hours of labor with your first child could charge you $135,000 for landing on Park Place without a trace of remorse.

"Well, all I know," I smiled, "is running has given me energy I never knew I had before. Even when I hit the wall, I know I can keep going."

"What wall is that?" he asked.

"You know that imaginary point where your legs feel like lead, your heart is ready to burst, your throat is dry, your mind no longer is capable of commanding your body, and all systems are running on automatic pilot. I've even had moments when I didn't even know what I was doing."

"You were tying your shoe," he said.

"Excuse me?"

"I've watched you. When you hit the wall, about five minutes out, you stop and tie your shoe."

He knew. "What gave me away?" I asked.

"No one runs with a handbag."

A WALTONS' CHRISTMAS

Saturday: 11:05 A.M.

"I need the phone," I said as I checked my watch nervously.

My daughter looked disgusted, gave her good-byes, and hung up.

"What's the emergency?"

"I always call Grandma at 11 every day. It will only take twelve seconds. Trust me," I said as I dialed.

"Mother, how's . . ."

Grandma: "Fever's down, cold gone. Instant relief. You?"

"One bedrm., l.r. to go. Going out?"

Grandma: "Yes."

"Dad?"

Grandma: "One birdie, one bogey, two beers. Serviceman arrive?"

"Negative."

Grandma: "Heard from B.R. Tues."

"Who's B.R.?"

Grandma: "Letter to follow. This is costing you a fortune. Love you."

"Ditto."

As I hung up, my daughter said, "That is the most incredible conversation I've ever heard in my life. What's the hurry?"

"Ever since Grandma found out I'm a toll charge and it cost 12 cents a minute to call here, she's been talking like a want ad."

"And you call her every day!" she said incredulously. "What do you have to talk about?"

Calling one's mother is a phenomenon few people can understand . . . unless they're a daughter. A need for your mother develops the day you come back from your honeymoon. I can honestly say I never knew Mother at all until Ma Bell came into our lives.

It took the daily phone call to learn that her secret pie crust came from a secret box in the supermarket. I had to discover by a slip of the tongue that she hid her billfold in the refrigerator in the vegetable crisper because only junk food addicts would rob a house in the first place and would never look under the lettuce.

One day she surprised me by commenting on how kissing on television bothered her. She said they always looked like they were chewing on a ham sandwich and bit down on a piece of fat they were trying to get out. Another time she admitted that when I was six months old she was bathing me and I fell off the table. She never told anyone in case I wasn't "right" and she didn't want to take the blame for it.

"Grandma's a neat lady," observed my daughter. "I think I always remember her best at Easter. Remember how she used to bake a lamb cake smothered in coconut with jelly bean eyes . . . and the cream-filled eggs three times our weight?"

"You bounced off the walls for three weeks. Then she started to hide hard-boiled eggs," I smiled.

"And after awhile she got a little fuzzy as to where she hid the eggs, and along about July or August when Granddad would cut the grass and grind up a three-month-old egg, it smelled like the bottom of a septic tank. It was Grandma's finest hour."

"I disagree. Grandma's finest hour is the parade of the boxes at Christmas."

"Is she still saving all those boxes every year?"

"You, who got a ring in a rectal thermometer box last year, have to ask that!" I said.

"Where does she store all of them?"

"You've seen her at Christmas. She's like a minesweeper. No sooner is the paper off the present than she is winding the ribbon around her fingers and smoothing the creases out of the wrapping paper. Then she stacks them like Russian dolls, takes them home to her closet, arranges them by size, and waits for all of us non-box savers to grovel.

"You should see her closet. If Tutankhamen's mother had a tomb, this would be it. You've never seen such a box glut in your life. One year I tried to borrow one of her boxes and she reminded me that I jammed an afghan in one the year before and broke down the sides. I said, 'Mother, I'm begging,' and as she handed one off the shelf said, 'Tell me what time it is to be opened and I'll be there.' "

"We talking Grandma?" said my son, joining us.

"Umm, we have to sit down sometime and figure out what we're doing Christmas."

"What's to figure out?" said my daughter. "We all come home Christmas Eve, decorate the tree, open the presents, eat ourselves into a coma, and it's all over."

"Wait a minute," said her brother. "Tell me Mom isn't planning another Walton Christmas." I tried to laugh with them, but the sound stuck in my throat.

"Admit it, Mom," said my daughter, "that had to have been not only the worst idea you ever had . . . but the worst Christmas in the history of holidays."

I remembered the exact moment the idea began to form . . .

It was Christmas night in 1979. I was under the tree and had just opened a box containing six shrimp forks. It was a gift to me from Harry. Harry was our puppy. My husband sat in a chair comatose watching "Bowling For Beers." Tinsel hung from his ears and lights circled his head. We had decided to leave him decorated through New Year's before we took him down.

A bird that we had plugged in to hear his light-hearted sound chirped every three seconds. I grabbed it by the throat and began choking it to death. The kids were riding cardboard boxes down the hill in the snow. The new sleds were under the tree.

I asked myself, "Is this what Christmas is all about?"

Is Santa Claus just a seasonal pitchman who arrives by helicopter, sells cat food, passes out samples of Monterey Jack in the supermarket, and hustles insurance to those fifty-five or over without a physical?

Has communicating with friends come down to the Christmas Newsletters Annual Barf-Off? Did I have to know that Elrod was sleeping dry at three weeks or that Estelle's ninety-year-old father just stiffened in her arms and died during dinner last summer?

And what about the fruitcake disciples who came out of the woodwork every December to have you put your hands on their 90-pound bricks of fruit, look skyward, and shout, "Hallelujah!"

Did anyone care that we ran ourselves ragged to compete with the woodworking teacher who lived next door who hoisted a large sleigh on his roof, had 500,000 lights surrounding his house, and was shown on the 11 o'clock news with traffic snaked back to the freeway?

How far would we go to satisfy the Goddess of Greed? Parents are such saps. Every year we gather our children around our knees and inquire, "What do you want for Christmas this year, Sweetheart?"

An infant who has no control over his bladder, is unable to feed himself, and cannot focus both eyes in the same direction says clearly, "I want the Rattell Pirate Ship, Catalog No. 90456, made of nontoxic superconstructed balsa and equipped with a two-masted square-rigger, a crew of fourteen, a dinghy, treasure chest, cannons, adjustable sails, working anchor, derrick for hoisting, and a crow's nest, cost $185. Don't accept a substitute. Look for the store in your area on channel 4."

I remember one year when all about me my friends had goals of working for peace and restoring America to a place of trust. You know what my goal was? Finding a doll for my daughter that drank milk, burped, rolled its eyes, said "I'm sleepy," and then deposited something very disgusting in its diaper.

When our children speak, we listen. When they cry, we start the motor of the car. When they threaten to stop breathing, we salivate, grow fur, and become predatory.

I was sick of rummaging through "kinky" little boutiques for my teenagers where I was the only person wearing shoes. Sick of being overdosed by incense and waited on by a guy with a ring in his nose and a tattoo of a snake on his tongue.

I grabbed a handful of tinsel and, lifting it with clenched fist, shouted, "I promise by all that is holy, I will never observe another Christmas without meaning."

By the time Christmas rolled around the next year, I was ready for it.

"Going to the cabin for Christmas is going to be wonderful," I said to my husband. "We can bake from scratch, light by candles, and heat by firelight, and what we don't have we'll live without."

"You have just described the Depression," he said dryly.

"I have just described the Waltons at Christmas. And look what a long run that family had. What made them so special was that they bought nothing. Every gift to one another was something they made with love and homemade paste. I bet there is creativity in this family that hasn't been discovered yet. Every gift exchanged this Christmas will be made from loving hands. The first thing I'm going to do when we get to the cabin is go through the forest, gather walnuts, and bake fruitcakes."

"You hate fruitcake."

"So, if no one eats them, we'll use them to extend the patio after Christmas."

There was no deterring me from my excitement to stage a noncommercial, back-to-basics Christmas that our family would remember the rest of their lives. In theory, it should have worked. I sent the boys out to chop down a live Christmas tree in the forest behind the cabin and set about creating those wonderful Christmas smells from the kitchen.

My mother dumped a glass of jelly in a saucepan. When I asked her why, she said she needed the glass to glue yarn around for a pencil holder. She reminded me the jelly cost $1.19, the yarn $1.50, and the glue $2.00, and for that she could have bought a gold-plated pen and pencil set from Bloomingdale's.

One child headed toward the bathroom with a bag of twine and a book, *How to Macramé*.

The boys returned in no time at all in a sheriffs cruiser. They did not have a permit to cut down a tree. The good news was that they were armed with a serrated bread knife so the ranger had not taken them seriously.

The smells were beginning to permeate the kitchen. Smells of wet paint and paste from unfinished gifts.

I sent the boys into town to buy a tree and set about decorating the cabin the old-fashioned way . . . the mantle with pinecones, and, on the tree outside the window, I hung some little birds I had bought in the dime store. I poured wax into milk cartons and popped corn to string for the tree.

The boys returned with a tree that looked quite ill. There was no "good side." We tried to simulate snow with paste and water and ended up throwing globs of it on the branches. It looked like a relief station for gulls. They ate the popcorn before it got to the thread.

I lit the homemade candles, which melted before I got the casserole to the table. My husband couldn't get the fire started. He was passing the hat begging for drivers' licenses and blank checks.

The dog ate a pinecone and was throwing up.

It started to rain, and the little birds I had put on the tree outside started to unravel. It looked like their intestines spilling out, and was not a festive sight.

Somehow I didn't remember the Walton kids sitting out in the car with the motor running with rock music on until midnight running down the battery.

This had to be the worst Christmas Eve of our lives.

And all I had wanted was to hear the chimes . . . like the little boy in the classic story who followed in the footsteps of kings and rich men who put gifts on the altar to hear the chimes ring out. The chimes were silent until he took off his coat and put it on the altar because it was all he had to give. It had been so long since I had heard them.

Early Christmas morning, I tiptoed out into the

living room. The fireplace was dark and cold. The tree was slipping away from us fast. The gifts were a ragtag collection of clumsily wrapped packages . . . some in newspapers, some in plastic bags.

The family drifted out and took their places on the sofa and the floor.

The first gift to be opened was from my husband to one of his sons, who was thinking of becoming a teacher. It was the only copy of his doctoral dissertation. It had taken him a year to write it.

My mother had painted a picture of the cabin on a piece of wood. She had just begun to paint during the past year.

There was a home-crafted bird feeder, wall plaques decorated with macaroni, crocheted bedroom slippers, and a recording of our family around the table at Thanksgiving that someone had made. There were shelled nuts, pillows, and dolls with yarn hair. And who will ever forget that dramatic moment when my son emerged from the bathroom with a macramé planter holder and hands that went with it because he didn't know how to end it?

Then, each of the kids produced an ornament they had made for the tree. A Christmas bulb out of cookie dough . . . a Styrofoam apple with a rubber worm coming out of it . . . and a small pie pan decorated with ribbon and a picture of the Blessed Mother and the Christ Child pasted on it.

As they hung them on the tree, the branches somehow became fuller and, from nowhere, a hundred lights seemed to sparkle. The fire in the fireplace took hold and suddenly burnt brighter, and the candles got a second life and glowed. For a second . . . and only a second . . . we not only found something we thought we had lost . . . but I heard chimes.

The clock in the living room brought me back to reality. It was noon.

"Can you believe Mom still has those crummy little ornaments we made?" said my daughter.

"And guess who gets their ornament on first?" said my son. The one who created the pie tin with a picture of the Blessed Virgin pasted inside, that's who. Every year, the best is first."

"Listen to him," said his brother. "You weren't first a couple of years ago. Those who don't come home for Christmas don't get a place on the tree."

"That's right," said his brother, "I was in the Peace Corps that year. How long ago was it?"

It was two years ago . . . and *that* was the worst Christmas we ever had. We were all together and yet we weren't all together.

My feelings were ambivalent and they confused me. Didn't we do everything right? Got his teeth straightened, his hernia repaired, his body packed with vitamins. Didn't we teach him how to parallel park, wipe his feet, put down lids, flush, feed himself, and make his own bed?

We gave him room to breathe, smiled in all the

right places, swallowed advice that lodged in our throats like a lump, and resisted spreading guilt.

When he left us at the airport, he could have been saying good-bye to a wrong number. "Don't worry, Mom. Worry makes you retain water."

We did all the right things. We encouraged them to take responsibility for their own successes and their own failures, develop their independence, and live their own lives. So, why at Christmas when they were gone did we feel so rotten?

And why did I fall apart when I hung on the Christmas tree that crummy little pie tin with a picture of the Blessed Virgin pasted inside dangling from a soiled ribbon?

"DON'T WORRY . . .
I'LL MANAGE"

"So, how's your life?" I asked my daughter as I started to make lunch. She grabbed the phone. "We've lost a roommate and if we don't get one to share the rent, we may have to sell our bodies, but don't worry, I'll manage."

As she dialed, I sat there stunned.

She listened more than she spoke. Finally, just before she hung up, she said, "I'm sorry, but it wouldn't work out. Good luck to you too."

"What's the problem? Was the rent too much?" I asked.

"No. On the surface she seemed perfect. A good job, loved to cook, considerate of people, no bad habits, her own car, and she can pierce ears."

"So, why didn't you ask her to move in?"

"We're looking for a size 10 with a steam iron."

"You're kidding," I laughed.

"Mom, getting roommates who are nice people just isn't enough. Last week I turned down a girl with her own VCR and downhill skis."

"Because . . . ?"

"She didn't own a steam iron. We thought we were onto one yesterday, but we were too late. They're picked off right away. Stereos are a dime a dozen. Everyone has her own system. But a steam iron. I cannot believe the bad luck we've had. First, our 'Mr. Coffee' lost her job and went back home. When we replaced her, our electric typewriter got married and split and we got stuck with a girl who said she was getting a suede jacket, but she just said that to get the room. Excuse me, just let me try to phone this one." I poured us both a cup of coffee as she talked.

"We'll get back to you," she said into the phone. "I'm not saying no. I just have to check it out with the others."

"A live one?"

"She's tempting. She doesn't have a steam iron, but she does have a cappuccino maker. Do you know how rare they are?"

"Aren't you being picky?"

"Look, we have our rules about the last roommate to join the group. She has to cook. Not just your ordinary cook, but a cook who can make a feast out of popcorn, two eggs, and three-day-old spareribs in a doggy bag.

"She must be rich, yet eccentric enough to love to do laundry.

"She must use the bathroom only in emergencies.

"She must be able to read lips over the din of a thousand decibels (equal to the noise of a jet hovering above the breakfast table).

"She must never sweat in borrowed clothes. That rule is not negotiable.

"She must never tie up the phone with trivia: making doctors' appointments, talking to Mother, etcetera.

"Any mature visitors to the apartment must give three weeks' notice."

"I'm curious," I said. "What did you bring to this better living through materialism arrangement?"

"Are you serious?" she laughed. "Two unmarried brothers. I could write my own ticket. No one has to know they're Neanderthals."

"So, how's your car? You mentioned something about the transmission."

"The car is dying. It gets two blocks to the gallon and I think the tailpipe is backing up noxious fumes into the car because I find I get very sleepy when I drive, but don't worry, I'll manage."

The cup shook in my hand. "That's terrible. Why don't you trade it in?"

"It's not that easy," she said. "Cars know when

you're ready to trade them in and they fall apart on you for revenge.''

"C'mon,'' I said, "you're not serious.''

"Remember a couple of years ago, I drove into a used car lot just to look . . . and the battery went dead? I bought a new one and wanted to get my money out of it, so I hung on. Then last year I put an ad in the paper and when this couple came over to look at the car, the tires turned bald in front of our eyes. I bought new tires and the car bought another year. Every time I even talk about new models, a knob falls off in my hand or the radiator boils over. I tell you it's weird. It knows.''

"What are you going to do?''

"There's a car dealer on the east side where they Se Habla Español. Pray the car isn't bilingual.''

"So, how much have you saved for a new car?''

"Who knows? My checkbook's screwed up. I wrote the bank a check to cover an overdraft and one of the managers wants me to come in. I think I'm going to prison, but don't worry, I'll manage. I think I'll approach it from the angle that bankers are people just like us who were young themselves once and can laugh at screw-ups.''

"You want an aspirin?'' I said as I opened the bottle.

"No. I hope I don't get the one who called me in before. He was terrible. He said he was entering me in the *Guinness Book of World Records* for writing 208 checks.''

"That *is* a lot.''

"In one week."

"My God."

"Under $2."

"Do I have to hear this?" I said.

"Without recording one of them."

"Well, at least you have a job," I said smiling thinly.

"I don't know how long. They said if I was late one more time, they'd terminate me and they wouldn't recommend I be hired again and I'd be doomed to the life of a recluse sitting around watching soaps and developing thunder-thighs, and I was late again yesterday, but don't worry, I'll manage."

"Why . . . why were you late?" I asked hesitantly.

"The doctor says I'm basically unhappy and I don't sleep. Once I get up late, my whole day falls apart. The buttons fall off my blouse, the hem on my skirt unravels, the soap falls in the drain and disappears, and the aerosol cans have a field day with me. Yesterday I shaved my legs with tub and shower cleaner, sprayed my hair with a deodorant that protected it for eighteen hours, and spritzed my pits with breath-freshener. I put my panty hose on backward, the elevator stopped on every floor, I forgot my billfold, and when I drove to the drive-in window, I got a flat tire."

"I'm sure everything will turn out . . ."

"You're not going to give me your struggle-builds-character speech, are you?"

"No, I was just trying to think of . . ."

"I've always known what the problem is. Genetics and placement in the family."

"What are you talking about?" I asked.

"From Dad's side of the family I got hair that wouldn't curl, frequent cold sores, and shoes that wear out on one side. You passed on to me limited motor skills and hopeless dependency. I didn't have a chance.

"I'm not blaming you, Mom, but I wish you wouldn't have led off with me in the family. Being the firstborn is a curse. You have no idea the pressure I have for setting standards, being disciplined beyond belief, and eventually having the responsibility for those who came after. Being perfect is *awesome*!"

"How soon you forget how we stood around applauding your B.M.s," I said. "We didn't do that for your brothers."

"That's the kind of pressure I'm talking about. Hey, what's done is done. Don't worry. I'll manage."

I sat there after she left wondering how I gave birth to a soap opera. If I had known thirty years ago what I knew now, maybe we'd have raised tomatoes. At least you could eat them.

You'd have thought someone would have told us that putting together a family is not for sissies. If it was adventure we were looking for, we could have flown a lawn chair over the Pacific propelled by balloons. If it was a desire to dedicate ourselves to service, we could have planted rice for the Peace Corps. If it was a "learning experience," we could have dropped in on a bunch of orangutans with a tape recorder.

Don't worry! I had done nothing else since we signed on for their education, health, entertainment, and moral and spiritual upbringing. Not a day went by that we weren't involved in some traumatic moment of their lives. At one time I even thought when they left home, I'd no longer have to worry about their problems. Hah!

I remember a couple of weeks ago. It was a Saturday and I could sleep until I got a headache. Nothing in the house leaked oil, dropped water, smoked when you plugged it in, made a funny sound, or had a light burnt out. The dog didn't look fat, and the big insurance premium was paid. The odds of all these things happening on the same day were the same as those of a middle-aged man admitting to hot flashes.

Then the phone rang.

One of my kids told me she was driving to Las Vegas and not to worry. Not to worry! Now I had to devote at least five hours to wondering if the car would break down and someone would rip off her money and a police officer would call and say, "I have someone here who wants to talk to you. Speak up. She's in traction."

Five hours of unrelenting fear that she would drop into a remote roadside tavern for a hamburger and be dragged out on the road by a motorcycle gang who did wheelies around her.

When the phone rang again, it was another child, who informed me he was going fishing in a rubber raft in the ocean. Why did they enjoy torturing their mother? I was going to wash my hair, but I canceled that in case a Soviet submarine surfaced just under their boat and dumped them into the Pacific. Or what if they caught a fish so gigantic it pulled their boat out into the open sea? Or what if Jaws III came to the beach or a tidal wave was on its way?

I calculated I had ten or twelve hours of worry ahead of me when my third child called. "Don't tell me, you're climbing Mt. Everest in tennis shoes."

"Actually, I'm staying home this weekend," he said.

I could not believe his insensitivity. Now I had to worry that he had no friends or social life. Unable to relate to anyone, he would become more withdrawn and finally trust no one. Eventually, he would pull his blinds and eat out of a saucepan on the stove and talk to a cat. I would never go to his wedding where everyone said, "She looks too young to be his mother." I would never dandle grandchildren on my knee where people would say, "She looks too young to have grandchildren."

And do they appreciate all this concern? They do not. They sit around and blame you for their shortness, for having a cowlick, for baldness, moles, and their place in the family.

It's a big price to pay for a romantic night, a bottle of cheap wine, and one reckless act.

THE GREED CYCLE

In the beginning children were taught the value of a nickel . . . and it was good.

They were taught they could earn a nickel by not crying and not playing with their gum and making tinkle. Little piggy banks were filled to overflowing. Some children could have owned property if they had been able to focus or write their own name.

Then they were introduced to the tooth fairy. And she was good.

The tooth fairy paid cash for fourteen teeth unless the tooth was placed under the pillow before the 15th or the 30th of the month. If this was the case, a check would be postdated at a local bank.

There were cost-of-living increases as the years went by.

The allowance was born and it was even better.

Children were paid to baby-sit themselves on New Year's Eve. Children got paid money for setting the table, not making the dog crazy, not allowing more than twenty kids at a time in the house, not losing the mail, and not tearing up the paper. Not letting the garden hose flood the yard cost extra and breathing was negotiable. With the allowance came the first financial phrase a child learns, "Do I have to use my own money?"

Then came the "No Pass–No Pay" legislation, which meant that if the child did not get a passing grade, parents would not give him money. There was a school in the Midwest with a falling enrollment that paid students to attend classes. And it was good again.

When children reached their teens, parents explained they could no longer sit on their assets. They had to look for a job. And it was . . . it was okay.

Children were cheered by the fact that Bill Walton got a million dollars a year for signing his name, Katherine Graham earned in excess of $375,000 and didn't even have to deliver the *Washington Post,* and the mayor of New York City made $88,000 a year by smiling and appearing on the 6 o'clock news.

They eventually settled for a job for minimum wage selling roofing over the phone.

Then came nepotism . . . and it was . . . not real good. A child was hired to help his dad paint the house and everything was to be on a strictly professional basis. His father told him what time to go to bed at night so he would be fresh in the morning. His mother routed him out and forced him to eat breakfast. Every fifteen minutes, his father would check to see if he had put drop cloths over the shrubbery and taken off the hardware around the windows.

Every time he got a phone call, his mother would tell them he joined the service and not to call anymore. She also checked his clothes to make sure he wasn't dripping paint before he could use the bathroom. He was paid with a postdated check that, if cashed on the date it was written, would incarcerate his parents for the next fifteen years.

And the kid paid taxes . . . and that was good for him.

When his dad asked for his W-2 form so he could declare him as an exemption, the child said, "Why would you want to do that?"

The father said, "Because for the last year we have fed, clothed, boarded, transported, indulged, and kept you in good health."

The child said, "Forget it! I'm filing separately so I can get a refund."

"But if we claim you, the government allows us an exemption right off the top. If we don't get that exemption, we're in a higher bracket."

The child said, "You should have thought of that

before you bugged me to go to work this summer. I wanted to stay here at home and visit with you and Mom and discuss my philosophy of life, but no, you weren't happy until I was out taking a job away from some unfortunate who needed it.''

It was hard to believe the child sold his parents down the river for a lousy $15.95 refund.

Then the child married and had a baby and one day Grandma pried open the little fist of the baby and pressed a nickel into it and the baby put it in its mouth to see if it was good. And it was. He held out his other hand and opened it for another nickel.

The greed cycle had begun again . . . and it felt good.

WHAT KIND OF CHILDREN WOULD BRING PARENTS INTO THIS WORLD?

Saturday: 2:20 P.M.

My friend Hazel pushed her way into the back door and paused cautiously.

There were thirty-five unwashed glasses on the countertop by the sink. The washer had a better pulse than I did. There were six cars in the driveway. A plastic bucket, a volleyball, and a stack of poker chips were in the middle of the table. The dog was eating beer nuts out of an ashtray. Newspapers turned to the theater section were strewn all over the kitchen. Pans dotted the stove, and from a distance radios blared.

"Either the kids are home or you have just been burgled."

"The kids are home," I said. "So, how have you been?"

"I was going to say 'fair,' but then I don't have a snake sitting on the hood of my car."

"I'm snake-sitting. Did I tell you our son is going back to school and is coming home to live?"

"That's one thing I can say about Russell," she said, pouring herself a cup of coffee. "He's independent. You wouldn't catch him living at home with us. After all, he *is* twenty-six years old!"

"Then he has his own apartment?"

"Apartment!" she snorted. "My dear, he has his own house. Dan and I figured we might just as well have equity in a home as pay rent on his apartment. I mean, at the end of all those years, what have you got to show for it except a bunch of rent receipts."

"You bought his home?" I gasped.

"It was the least we could do," she said. "After all, where was he going to put all that furniture he carted away for the last eight years? It has all worked out perfectly. Just when we made the last payment on his car, his lease was up on the apartment."

"You bought his car?"

"How else could he get to his father's plant? We originally bought him a motorcycle, but those things are so dangerous. When we paid his insurance premiums, they told us because he rode a motorcycle he was a high risk. We couldn't afford that kind of rate."

"Then you pay his insurance."

"Only his car, Dear, and his health. I mean, what are kids supposed to do these days? Most of them can't even afford to be sick. We figured insurance was safer than taking a chance on being hit with a hospital bill cold turkey. Especially since he's taking some night classes and burning the candle at both ends. We do the best we can with his food, utilities, and the new baby coming."

"Russell is married?"

"For the second time. Believe you me, it's not true that two can live as cheaply as one. The girl eats like a horse. But she's much nicer than the one we pay alimony to. Now there's a piece of work. I worry about Russell, I really do. All that responsibility. The future so iffy. But it's like Dan and I told him, 'You have to get out of the nest and stand on your own two feet sometime.' If you don't mind a piece of advice, boot your son out. You'd be doing him a favor, and it's the only way he's going to know what independence is all about. He'll either sink or swim!"

"It's a whole new ballgame, isn't it, Hazel?" I said, folding up the newspapers. "Manners, morals, values, everything is so different from when we were first married."

"Isn't that the truth," she said. "Did you hear where health insurance companies are thinking of cutting down on the cost of birth by paying new mothers to leave the hospital early?"

"How early?" I asked.

"If you leave within twenty-four hours after delivery, they'll pay you from $50 to $200."

It took awhile for the shock of what she had told me to take effect. From a woman who clutched her bedsprings for thirty days after the birth and then had to be evicted physically, I couldn't believe what I had just heard. Every woman knows once you turn in your paper slippers, they put you in a pair of track shoes and a T-shirt with a red S on it and you hit the ground running.

Why, giving birth is the last stronghold women have for getting any consideration. This is your day in the sun . . . maybe your last one. You have given the ultimate gift to your husband, who takes everything else back and credits it to your account. You have fulfilled your mother's dreams of revenge. You have given your father a picture to replace Debbie Reynolds in his billfold. You have enough stretch marks to spread guilt for two fur coats, a quartz watch, and a trip to St. Croix in January. We just gave birth to a quintessential headache and now they want to buy us off.

"There's a real contradiction here," I said to Hazel. "Men think nothing of putting their car in the shop for three days until they can get parts. They stand in line, wrapped in a blanket, for forty-eight hours to get World Series tickets. They understand a bank that needs two days to clear a check. But they're ready to go for instant birth. Just add heavy breathing and simmer for twenty-four hours."

"I think they ought to at least wait until the sedative wears off," said Hazel.

"How long was that for you?" I asked.

"About three years."

"Well, at least you have Russell married. I can't get mine off the dime. When it comes to marriage, they speak another language. Would you be shocked if I told you my husband and I had never had a meaningful conversation in our entire lives? I don't even know what it is."

"It probably has calories," sighed Hazel.

"And marriage contracts. What kind of a way is that to start a marriage . . . dividing up the money before you've made it, the house before you've furnished it, and the kids before you've conceived them? All this talk about the new sexual freedom. How does that differ from the old sexual freedom? And why do they need a manual for it? You're lucky, Hazel. Your son saw something in you to emulate."

"Don't rush it. It's a real trip. For Russell's first wedding, we spent $5,000. They split the same week the wedding proofs faded."

"But he got a nice girl this time around?" I asked, hopefully.

"He met her on a beach in California. She sat around in bib overalls and played the guitar and ate passion fruit. She had no idea how to turn on a stove, and the closest she ever came to domesticity was a plastic fork tucked in her headband. When my son asked her to marry him, she spoke her first words to me, 'Gift Registry.' I've never seen such a list. I ask you, where would a girl like that learn words like Wallace, Wedgwood, and Waterford? We sold off some stocks and bought her a pickle fork for a wedding present.''

"Things do change," I sighed. "Is it my imagination or are the babies doing the diaper commercials getting older? I saw one the other day that spoke lines and looked old enough to prepare its own formula. Toilet training doesn't seem as important to today's mothers as it was to us. Maybe they have more important things to do.''

"You talk about babies in diapers getting older," snorted Hazel. "Have you seen some of the new mothers lately? They're getting a little long in the tooth.''

"I've always felt there are two things a woman should never do after the age of thirty-five: stand in natural light and have a baby," I said.

"They probably think it's a lot of fun to have a baby who will sit around and connect liver spots on Mommy's arms, but in reality, there are a lot of problems older mothers haven't even considered. For example, just when Baby is outgrowing his need for naps, Mommy will need them, and when his teeth start coming in, Mommy's will start falling out.''

"True," I nodded, "and the worst adjustment will be when the babies get to be teenagers. If a mother has a child at the age of thirty-five, she will be fifty-one years old when her son starts to drive at age sixteen. Anyone knows that at that age it's too late for a mother to develop patience and too early for her to die.''

"Trust me," said Hazel, "it's only a matter of time before older mothers are racing their kids for the baby food. Sometimes I feel sorry for this generation. I think they're really screwed up.''

"They sure seem to know everything there is to know about sex. Did you know that more people make love on Sunday than on any other day of the week? Or that the peak hours are 10 P.M. to 7 A.M.?''

"Who cares?" said Hazel.

"Or that more women sleep next to the wall than men and that men wearing boxer shorts are more likely to become fathers?''

"Give me a break.''

"Hazel, we burn 150 calories making love, which is just under throwing a Frisbee, which burns 200 calories.''

"And here's one for you," said Hazel. "Garlic is still the most effective form of birth control.''

"I was being serious," I said.

"So am I, and I say it's hogwash. If you believe kids today have smarts about sex then you'll believe that Cathy Rigby invented puberty. Can you imagine how much a child knows about sex after watching soaps for most of his life? It's a false picture. A child can be born within six weeks after conception and be married before the year is up. If it is a long-running series, it could take only three months for a full-term baby. However, in a three-part miniseries last year, three births occurred, including twins who were born three weeks apart when they were preempted by a baseball play-off.''

''I never thought of that.''

''Young people don't know what to believe anymore. Eggs don't produce babies. They hatch panty hose. Women don't carry babies where they're supposed to. They have Jordache pregnancies. Love isn't a reason to have a baby . . . sagging ratings are.''

''You should hear my mother talk about kissing on television. Whenever a hero used to kiss a heroine, it looked like a tribute to Mt. Rushmore. Nowadays it's an aerobics exercise.''

''Isn't that the truth,'' said Hazel. ''What was it Henry Fonda called it in *On Golden Pond?*''

''Sucking face.''

''Ummm, be honest,'' she said. ''Does it really titillate you?''

''Not really. I just sit there and wonder where all of Joan Collins' lipstick goes . . . or if one of them has a bad back.''

''Sometimes,'' said Hazel, ''I watch all the fuzzy fade-ins and fade-outs and obscure overlaps and try to figure out what part of the body is being shown. And the heavy breathing!''

''I can hear the same thing when I ask my husband to move the sofa,'' I said.

''The problem with kids,'' said Hazel, ''is you

can't tell 'em anything. I read where some high school teacher in the Midwest tried to simulate married life in his classroom. He had the kids pair off and gave them an income and a budget.''

''What happened?''

''Well, each pair of students was supposed to give birth to an egg. They named it, decorated it, housed it, and figured out how they were going to raise it. He even had them take the egg home, and one of them was required to attach it to a big toe by a string to show them how constant raising a child is.''

''Did it work?'' I asked.

''Well, they found out you can do a lot of things to make eggs look different. You can paint them in different colors, decorate them with gold, put them in a satin-lined bed or a bed made of pencil shavings, but underneath they are pretty much the same. They found they looked fragile, but a couple of them were dropped and cracked and they still survived. But at least it gave 'em a taste of the 'real world.' Hey, I gotta run. Talk to you tomorrow.''

I closed the door and mechanically began to pick up glasses and carry them to the sink. The ''real world.'' How many times had I threatened our kids with it? I told 'em it was a jungle, a place where you can count your friends on one hand, a future existence where you won't have your parents to kick around anymore.

The ''real world.'' When our son was nine, a group of boys shoved his head into a paper towel dispenser in a theater rest room and demanded his money. We had sent him to a Disney movie because we didn't want him to see violence.

When our daughter was sixteen, her best friend was killed one night by a drunk driver.

When a son was twelve, his bicycle was stolen, which he bought with his own money. The policeman said, "Tough. You should have locked it."

When one of our sons went to camp, his best friend was black and he heard the word "nigger" and saw firsthand the ugliness of prejudice.

In their short lives they had known rejection, discrimination, life-threatening sickness, fear, disappointment, violence, and pain.

The "real world." Why didn't I tell them it was a myth? From the day they entered it . . . slippery and warm and complacent . . . they were smacked on the behind to fill their lungs with cries of annoyance, shock, and rage. How much more real can it get than that!

WHAT ARE FRIENDS FOR?

Their world started out small enough. It encompassed an area from the bedrooms to the gate on the basement steps. They were certainly cloistered enough, seeing only parents, siblings, relatives, and an occasional visitor from the outside.

It might have remained that way had it not been for the fact that it was my world too, and I was beginning to talk to the tropical fish.

I needed a surrogate mother . . . someone who would sit with my children in my absence and bring to them the same high standard of care, intelligence, and integrity. A special person dedicated to preparing them for their places in society.

I found all of that in "Debbie," an eleven-year-old with braces who had no social life and could make change for a $50 bill at 3 in the morning. She was to be the first of many baby-sitters who could show our children that authority could be fun and profitable.

The kids were present when I interviewed her. "Debbie," I said (they were all named Debbie), "I'm going to ask you a few hypothetical questions just to make sure you can handle any situation that may arise as a baby-sitter. First, tell me what you would do if a child refused to go to bed."

"I would threaten to eat him!" she said, blowing a large bubble from her gum.

"Very good. Now, how much liquid do you give a child younger than six before putting him to bed?"

"When they complain of being thirsty, you mist the plants on their window sill and tell them to inhale deeply."

"Wonderful," I nodded. "Now, here's a toughie. What do you do when one of your charges pushes a coin up his nose?"

She thought a moment. "What denomination is the coin?"

"A dime."

"For a dime," she said, "I wouldn't lose my place in the book I'm reading. For a bill, I might get out the vacuum sweeper and suck it out."

The kids cheered and I hired their first prime-time surrogate mother.

I have to admit, she became the most important person in my life too. Gynecologists and hairdressers came and went, but if Debbie got a date or had plans, I didn't want to live anymore. Getting ready for her visit was $3 short of a wedding. The house had to be picked up. The soft drinks were iced, snacks set out, the TV set adjusted, and kids threatened and stashed away in their rooms. I tipped Debbie for staying awake. I tipped her for answering the phone. I tipped her for returning empties to the carton.

In fact, I remember the very day she discovered there was more to life than "don't forget to flush" and Winnie the Pooh. It was a Wednesday. In the prime of her life, she was struck down by puberty, a condition requiring a social life. We never saw Debbie again, but she made an impact on the lives of my children.

As their world got bigger, so did the circle of friends who were absorbed into our lives . . . the steady stream of sleep-overs and eat-overs— children who played musical chairs and beds throughout the neighborhood.

Usually, there was no warning of their visit. You would be calling the family to dinner and shutting off the oven when your child would say, "Can Stanley (Jack, Joanie, Gloria, residents of the free world) stay for dinner?"

There's an entire generation out there today who believe Mrs. Bombeck serves half-macaroni and half-spaghetti with sauce so pale it wouldn't stain a tablecloth—and chicken parts that aren't identifiable even to another chicken.

Sometimes, I was faced with a critical food shortage during a surprise guest attack and put my FHB (Family Hold Back) plan into action.

It always reminded me of a brilliant story told by the late humorist, Sam Levenson. Sam was one of eight children and "company" had its privileges. Before the meal, his mother told the kids, "When the meat is passed around say, 'No thank you. I'm not hungry,' so our guest won't think he's taking the food out of our mouths." It worked, but when dessert was served, his mother sailed it quickly by the kids, saying, "You didn't eat your dinner! So you don't get dessert!"

Without fail, every time I was having pork chops, the kids invited a friend to dinner. There is nothing you can do to make a pork chop look bigger. I've tried. I've breaded them so that the egg fans out two inches on all sides, tucked dressing around them like a skirt, and arranged them on a saucer, but they still look like what they are . . . not enough pork chops. Sometimes I think there should be an award to honor the acting ability of a mother who sits at the table nibbling on a bone sandwich and feigning fullness.

It always amazed me that I cooked 738 meals a year, packed 1,040 lunches, made 2,055 snacks and 30 special banquets for birthdays and holidays, and if a friend refused to eat something, the family would turn on me like a bunch of vigilantes.

"Why do you serve those stupid things that roll around a plate?" (Peas.) "Do we have to eat those slimy sticks that swell up when you start to chew them?'' (Asparagus.) "I know those lumps are yucky, but if you hold your breath and swallow them, they'll disappear.'' (Onions.)

I'll never forget an ungrateful teenager who was the guest of our daughter. "Try these cookies,'' she was told, "they've made Mom a legend.''

The girl bit into one and made a face. "The apple did the same for Eve,'' she said.

Eventually, persons from the outside exude influence over your children's destiny, which brings to mind Miss Marpling, the children's piano teacher.

I hadn't thought of her in years until I ran into her in a department store dining room a few weeks back. I must say I was surprised. She looked wonderful. The nervous twitches around her mouth were gone. The eyes that used to spin counterclockwise in her head were steady now and held my gaze. And I realized she was smiling. I had never seen her smile before—even at recitals.

"Miss Marpling,'' I said, "how long has it been?''

She took a deep breath. "Eleven years, two months, one week, and three days.''

"And are you still placing those pudgy little sticky fingers on the piano keys? Goodness gracious, do you have any idea how many little people you had marching to the tune of your metronome?''

"You still blame me, don't you?'' she said.

"Don't be ridiculous," I said. "Do you honestly think I still go to pieces every time I hear 'There's a Rose in the Bottom of My Teacup'? When the doctor explained to me it was just a child's way of working out parental hostility, I understood it."

"Mrs. Barnhardt blames me," she said bitterly.

"That was different. You had absolutely no right to assign 'Lady of Spain' to a beginning accordion student for a recital. I hear she still isn't right."

As I ate lunch, I occasionally cast a glance at Miss Marpling and a wave of affection came over me. What had she done that was so wrong? She took three children off my hands for an hour every week and introduced them to the "March of the Little Toy Soldiers" (to be played lively), the "Parade of the Turtles" (to be played softly), and "The Yodeler and His Echo" (to be played in the basement in Kansas City, Mo.).

She awakened a talent . . . if not for making music, then for appreciating it.

She taught them what instruments can do and how you can play softly for effect or louder when you place your foot on the pedal.

She taught them if you practiced for three lousy hours on the same song and hit the same stupid note every time, you could turn your mother into a sniveling bowl of cookie batter.

I wasn't the only one. Mothers of musicians everywhere live out their lonely lives in desperation. God love 'em. They never know when a phone is ringing. They never hear a jet zooming overhead. They don't hear anything after awhile. They just sit there with a smile on their faces, watch lips, and pick up an occasional word here and there.

They want to believe that Mozart had a mother. They want to believe Mrs. Osmond lived in a hotel while her children were growing up and practicing on their instruments.

They are the loneliest women in the world, apologizing to neighbors, to other members of the family, to the world. They are torn between having the patience to hear "The Spider Song" on the piano for five hours at a crack or strangling a tuba player with their bare hands and feeling guilty for the rest of their lives.

It is usually the fathers who encourage a talent that is so dormant in their children, it takes x-rays to find it. It was my husband who suggested we give all three of our children piano lessons. I did that. One day he said, "When are we going to get a piano for them to practice on?"

"That wasn't part of the deal," I said. "I only said yes to the lessons. After all, if they played baseball, would we turn our living room into a sandlot?"

He bought the piano anyway and was sorry when the sound turned his lawn brown.

Miss Marpling did not look well and I thought, life is so short, why not let bygones be bygones? As I left, I dropped by her table to tell her so when she grabbed my hand and said, "I forgive you for your three little no-talent children."

By the time your children are dating, your contribution to their lives is minimal. There comes the parade of the Twinkies and the Neanderthals . . . all potential in-laws. I'll always remember the first one to be brought "home." Her beauty was flawless. She was built like an inflatable. She brought me a live poinsettia. She was bright and funny and smart and had read all of my books. She opened her mouth, and I knew she was wrong! wrong! wrong! for my son. She had an overbite.

I took her aside and said, "Darling, you may think you are attracted to my son, but underneath that even row of teeth and those healthy gums is a very ordinary person. Believe me."

It sounded harsh, but you have to know those straight white teeth in my son's mouth represent my cruise to Norway, my matching set of Vuitton luggage, and my operation for a deviated septum. (What is there to breathe for when your child eats like a beaver?) They represent five years and $6,500 worth of payments.

With every Eddie Haskell . . . every sleep-over . . . every friend you approve or disapprove of, we lose a little more of the child to them. They are ultimately shaped and molded by everyone who touches their lives.

When we moved away from the old neighborhood, I observed the most agonizing, heart-wrenching scene in my entire life. My son was saying good-bye to his best friend. The two had been inseparable. They ate together, slept together, played together, and were together on family vacations. I once took the kid shopping for school clothes before I remembered he wasn't mine. There were embarrassing tears that day and clumsy good-byes with promises to write and always keep in touch. He was family!

Several years passed when my son returned to the old neighborhood for a visit. He could hardly wait to see his old friend. He caught up with him on a Saturday afternoon shooting baskets in the gym.

"Well?" we asked.

"He didn't remember me," said my son.

He learned something that day. Friends are "annuals" that need seasonal nurturing to bear blossoms.

Family is a "perennial" that comes up year after year, enduring the droughts of absence and neglect.

There's a place in the garden for both of them.

IT'S 11 O'CLOCK. DO YOU KNOW WHERE YOUR PARENTS ARE?

Saturday: 4:40 P.M.

Hello, Jeff, guess who? Yeah, I'm home for the weekend. Dad took another one of his infamous pictures for the Christmas card, and Mom is doing her Donna Reed number. Believe me, it isn't easy raising parents these days. You never hear about that. All people talk about is how hard it is to raise kids. Well, I'm here to tell you parents are no day at the beach. They just got better P.R. You hear a lot about the teenage driver, but what have you heard about the menopausal mother on the passenger side? You climb in the car and she says, 'Mother trusts you to be a responsible adult when it comes to operating this vehicle. I know you will not do anything rash and will do exactly as I say. Just relax, and remember that one careless mistake on your part and you could maim your mother for the rest of her life.' She's got another cute trick. You'll be riding along and all of a sudden, you hear her sucking in her breath, grasping the dashboard with both hands, and making a guttural, inhuman sound. When you ask what's the matter, she grabs her chest and whispers, 'Nothing.' Something happens to parents when their kids become teenagers. They are struck down with some kind of premature senility. They don't know anything. There was a time they could make a traffic light turn green by blowing on it, and they were never at a loss for an answer to a question like, 'How come God never married?' but all of a sudden they become repetitious.

I even had to correct my mother's grammar in front of company. Boy, the night when she couldn't remember that my sister got to lick the pan of chocolate batter when she was three and I had to wait until I was five, I lost all respect for her. She said to me one night, 'Why don't you get off my case and stop prosecuting me?' I hated to spell p-e-r-s-e-c-u-t-i-n-g in front of her, but someone had to tell her. Around that age, they seem to resist change. I cannot believe Mom drove to a self-service gas station and tried to force the leaded nozzle into an unleaded gas tank. She doesn't think. After she corrected the mistake, she went to pay her bill and the clerk said, 'You owe seven cents on pump no. 23.' She said, 'I didn't put that gas in my car.' 'What did you do with it?' asked the clerk. 'I poured it on my foot. I meant to pour the unleaded.' 'On your foot?' 'In the car.' The whole thing was embarrassing. I'm worried about parents. I really am. They don't seem to have any focus for their lives. The other night, all of us kids were sprawled out all over the living room with a stack of videocassettes, eating and having a good time, and we caught them splitting. We asked, 'Where are you going?' They said, 'Out.' 'Out where?' 'Just out.' We said, 'Do you know what time it is? It's time when most people are going to bed. The only thing you can get into at this hour is trouble. They said they were just going to bum around. My sister said, 'I don't know why you can't just spend one night at home once in awhile and watch television with us. Would it kill you?' They said, 'It's boring. Besides, you never watch our shows.' We said, 'We'd watch them if you didn't watch those trashy things on PBS with the English accents.' We told them to be home early, but we were up half the night waiting to hear the motor turn off and know they were home safe. I don't enjoy nagging at them all the time, but they're so darned frustrating. You can talk to them and you think they're listening, and the next morning, they're doing something stupid. When my mother was younger, she used to be neat as a pin. You should see her office now. The plants are dead. There are coffee cups with the coffee dried up in them sitting around all over the place and a wastebasket that is ready to walk. I said to her the other day, 'When was the last time this ironing board was down?' She said, 'In 1971. The year we moved.' I informed her I was embarrassed to death to have people come in the room and she said, 'Then shut the door. It's my room and they have no business in here.' I'll tell you the truth. I'll be glad when Mom and Dad get their own apartment. Nice talking to you, Jeff.''

"YOU LOOK WONDERFUL"

I wouldn't admit it to anyone, but having the family around always makes me feel . . . old. Maybe it's the way everyone has started to say "You look wonderful" instead of hello.

I liked it better when they asked, "How's it goin'?" or "What have you been up to?" But "You look wonderful" sounds like they're reassuring me. It seems so insincere . . . maybe because people say it whether you've just rolled out of bed or the recovery room. Come to think of it, at a funeral I attended last week, the same people who hugged me and said, "You look wonderful," peered into the coffin and remarked, "She looks wonderful!" No wonder it makes me suspicious.

To make matters worse, I pull on a sweater and

my mother's arm comes through the sleeve. The physical transformation is the least of it. I'm doing all the things she used to do that used to drive me crazy. I save twist ties from bread wrappers by the pound. When I get into the car, I don't even turn on the motor until I check all the mirrors and the position of the seat and arrange my dress.

I can hear water dripping a half-mile from the house, and I can't stand to be near a sweater without picking it up and folding it like they do in department stores.

It's only a matter of time, I guess, before I put a fake flower on the antenna of my car at the shopping center. I used to be so fun-loving, so impetuous, so impractical. I'd wash my hair at midnight and go outside in the winter without socks. Now I tell my kids that an unmade bed gives you bad skin!

Who was the idiot five years ago who said, "I'm proud of my age. I earned every wrinkle?" That idiot was me. No one has wrinkles anymore. They have plastic surgeons. Even that funeral I went to last week. You couldn't tell if the deceased was going or coming. It probably wouldn't take that much to make some changes . . . especially for someone with a little creativity.

Silicone injections to reduce forehead furrows ($275) and forehead lifts to correct drooping eyebrows, bags, and sags ($3,000). Home solution: move out before son moves back home.

Cryosurgery, the freezing to remove raised and

flat brown age spots from hands ($100 an office visit). Home solution: connect the liver spots and palm them off as mesh gloves.

Chin lift to eliminate double chin and to lift and tighten chicken-neck throat ($2,500). Home solution: wear turtleneck sweaters.

Chemical peeling to erase laugh lines around eyes and mouth ($500). Home solution: buy an untrained puppy. You will never laugh again.

It's not just a matter of looking older . . . I feel older. Is it because I see my past in my children? Have I given up center stage and become a bit player with fewer lines every year? Are they a reminder of what I was?

I know this. I will never go to another high school or college reunion as long as I live. It's too depressing. Everyone wants to look like he or she is twelve again. Everyone wants to be the one who fulfilled the class prophecy.

Who needs it? What did they ever do for me? Taught me how to diagram a sentence and conjugate three Spanish verbs. Big deal. Some people are staples at every reunion and wouldn't miss it for the world. Every year they suck it in and play the game of beat the clock.

You always see insurance salesmen. To them, one class reunion is worth 500 callbacks. Show them a picture of your family and from somewhere they pull out an artist's brush and take Daddy out of the picture, leaving you with no income and a

$130,000 mortgage. They really know how to liven up a party.

Old cheerleaders always show up . . . the ones whose bust measurement exceeds their I.Q. by 35. You can't miss a cheerleader. She has the only chest that takes two name tags. If Sandra Day O'Connor appeared in her black robe, the cheerleader would say, "How many children do you have now and where are you living? Honey, you ought to be color-draped. You're definitely an autumn—not black!"

You can count on seeing rich people who used to be poor. They drive new cars, give you their "card," and hide out in the rest room from the university development fund-raisers. Same thing with shy people who have their own syndicated talk shows. Their motive in returning is revenge upon all the teachers who never called on them when they knew the answer and were too shy to raise their hands.

Maybe if I hit it big in Amway, I'd go back but . . .

Something is changing within me. I can feel it. Every time I buy something of value, I have visions of my kids marking it down to $2 at a garage sale. Sometimes I wake up at night in a cold sweat just thinking that my cup and saucer collection will fall into the hands of someone furnishing a summer cabin who doesn't mind dishes that don't match.

I don't mean to frighten or depress anyone. Lord knows I'm not "going anywhere" tomorrow, but I felt a sense of order about doling out some treasures to my kids last summer. I can still see the look of surprise on my daughter's face as I held out my seventeen-year-old mink stole and said, "Do you know what this is?"

She put on her glasses and came in for a closer look. "Help me," she said.

"Christmas. Severely depressed. Family. Daddy. Surprise."

She nodded. "I got it. Daddy killed this and we ate it for Christmas dinner."

"It was my first mink coat," I said, "and now it's yours."

She was so overcome, she was speechless.

"There are so many priceless bits of memorabilia in my possession, I hardly know where to begin," I said. "I want to be fair to you and your brothers. There's a glass lid that belonged to a cast-iron skillet given to me by my grandmother. The skillet's lost, but the lid doesn't have a crack in it. No sense having some attorney rip it off."

During the ensuing weeks, I dispersed a hand-blown glass sea urchin I bought at Disneyland, a coconut shell necklace from Hawaii, and an old piece of sheet music from their piano-playing days.

I parted with my high school class ring and a clothespin painted like a pig that holds a recipe. When my son dropped by, I handed him a box and smiled. "We have only our todays."

He said, "Is this another 'living bequest'?"

"I hand-hooked this little rug for your nursery,"

I said, unrolling it on the floor. "Do you remember the little sailboat and the seagulls?"

"I remember," he said solemnly.

"Do you remember that it took your mother twelve years to finish at an expense of $140 . . . $90 in yarn alone?"

"Why don't you hang on to it, Mom," he said. "You've got a few good years left."

Two weeks later I saw the rug in his apartment. It was lining the dog bed.

Maybe Elizabeth Taylor is right. Age is inevitable and we should welcome it like an old friend. It's a fact that the world spins on the energy of its young. That's why I have a priest who smells like Clearasil and a doctor who wears Calvin Klein jeans on his daily rounds.

There was a time when the stewards on planes looked like they had just landed their first job. Now the men piloting the planes are looking forward to shaving for the first time.

And Lord, what I would give to see a mature woman delivering the 6 o'clock news! Sometimes I think if I see another silken-haired beauty queen with capped teeth and wet lips wrapped around the failing economy, I'll scream.

I passed a mirror and mechanically pulled up my jowls and chins. It could be worse. Maybe Mother had passed her cellulite down to me, but my grandmother had left me a greater legacy: her! For years I watched my Grandma baste her roots, pound her body, and pat her chin in an effort to bring the aging process to its knees.

She succeeded. She was like a Timex watch that you could bury in sand, spin around, sink, beat on, misplace or drop, and she still kept right on ticking until the day she died.

I remember when she was in her seventies she went to the nursery one day and bought a five-gallon blue spruce tree. The nurseryman said, "Are you aware these only grow less than an inch a year?"

Grandma said, "So, when they get higher than the house, I'll have 'em trimmed."

It's funny. When my mom and dad were my age, I thought about hiring someone to feed them. And now . . . I positioned myself in front of the mirror again . . . now, *My God! My husband and I are beginning to look alike!* I had never noticed it before, but we have the same firm jaw when the red light goes on in the car in downtown traffic. We both chew the inside of our mouths when an accountant calls. We both roll our eyes to the ceiling when a speaker says, "There are fourteen major points I'd like to share with you."

Without even realizing it, we have blended. His hair got longer; mine got shorter. His hands softened; mine hardened. He grew a stomach; I grew upper arms. His chest grew with exercise; mine dropped to my knees. My chins came from chocolate, his came from sleeping in a chair, but they're the same chins.

And we not only finish sentences for each other, we don't even have to start them. Just yesterday morning, we were both reading the paper when I asked, "Are you going again this year?"

He answered, "What's the point?"

I said, "You'd think Reagan would issue a statement on . . ."

He said, "He did. Finish the story. You need anything while I'm out?"

I said, "Why do you go to the same store all the time? You know they never have . . ."

He said, "They did last week and you didn't want any."

I said, "Do you think we're beginning to . . ."

He said, "Not a chance."

"Then how come you . . ."

"Coincidence."

Maybe age is kinder to us than we think. With my bad eyes, I can't see how bad I look, and with my rotten memory, I have a good excuse for getting out of a lot of stuff. I can't remember where the fuse box is located, what weight of oil goes into the car, and how I'm supposed to record checks in the checkbook. Besides, it's the one thing that holds us together. He relates to a woman who stands in front of an open refrigerator and wonders why, and I relate to a man who walks to the other end of the house and stands in the room muttering, "What did I come back here for?"

And he always supplies missing words to my

sentences, like Ed Asner, croissant, James Michener, and artichoke.

I guess there are a couple of ways you can handle time. You can be like my grandmother, who regarded it as a formidable foe in a game of wits where one wins and the other one loses. Or you can have respect for one another and live in reasonable harmony in a give-and-take situation.

I caught another glance in the mirror. My knees had grown together, my laugh lines were deep enough to plant barley, oats, or rye, and wicker chairs were painful. I was part of a natural evolution of things where children begat the future, earning me a place in the past.

As I took a deep breath, I saw my father's face reflected in the mirror next to mine. He said, "You look wonderful! Honest!"

"Don't say that."

"You don't want me to tell you you look wonderful?"

"Tell me something I can believe," I said. "I feel like I'm in the soufflé of my life and someone just slammed the door."

"You should complain," he said. "I just said to a clerk in the supermarket, 'I'm ready to check out,' and she said, 'We all have to go sometime, Gramps.' "

IF A HOME IS A MAN'S CASTLE . . . LET HIM CLEAN IT

Saturday: 5:15 P.M.

In the media room, my dad held his cup as I poured coffee into it. "What are you doing out shopping? I thought you were retired."

He lowered his voice to a whisper. "Someone's got to keep the house running," he said. "Your mother would let everything go to pot. Do you have any idea what I found in the refrigerator last week? A cake of yeast that had expired June 17. If I had run my business like she runs that house, I'd have been bankrupt."

My father. I cannot remember the day I dropped the prefix "step" from his title. I referred to him as my dad and it seemed right somehow.

How long had it been since he came into the game of parenting as a relief pitcher? Usually everyone loves a man who comes in when the team is in trouble, the bases are loaded, and someone is needed to win the game.

But a stepfather does the same thing and is accused of "interfering."

Take a substitute teacher. He's kinda naïve and new and goofs up a lot and has a whole class rooting for him, but a stepfather is a substitute and he's "stupid."

And don't we cheer on the understudy who hops in at the last minute and gives a performance with no experience? Everyone sitting there in the darkness is hoping to witness the birth of a new star, but a stepfather is "trying to take the real star's place."

Families aren't easy to join. They're like an exclusive country club where membership makes impossible demands and the dues for an outsider are exorbitant.

Thank God, he hung in there.

"You see," he continued, "I'm trying to ease your mother out of going to the supermarket. She's totally inefficient. Can you imagine spending $16 a minute and not having a list? The woman never reads a label to find out what's in the can. Just grabs it off the shelf. Why, they could be using pig lips in it for all she knows."

As Dad continued his tirade, I thought to myself, there are two things a woman should do by herself . . . give birth and shop. I have been with my own husband to the store a few times. He always stands around on one leg like a napping whooping crane. Men never really understand that shopping is meant to be a spontaneous, impulsive, madcap adventure.

I'd be halfway down the second aisle before I realized he was on the first aisle trying to fix the wheel of the shopping cart.

"You can't use this cart," he'd say. "The wheels all go in a different direction." Women shoppers would just look at him and shake their heads.

He drove me crazy with a pocket calculator, figuring out I could save one cent per ounce by buying a liquid bleach. In between his comparison shopping, he would arrange the cart, putting all the taxables in one corner, the dairy products in another, and surrounding the eggs by a wall of toilet tissue.

Someone did a study of men in supermarkets and discovered they're just too weird. They rarely shop in tennis clothes, stand around and gossip, or spend more money than they have. They never squeeze anything in produce, or buy trees, underwear, or cassette recordings. They never figured out that if spending $16 a minute isn't fun . . . then what is?

I honestly never thought my father would become domesticated.

He was a man who couldn't push down the tab

on the toaster and thought aspic was a ski lodge in Colorado. The day after he retired, he was speaking yellow wax buildup like a native and running the entire house.

Looking back, I think it all began when he joined the liberated men of the eighties . . . those patron saints of sacrifice who "make the coffee in the morning."

It's all he talked about. To him, "making coffee in the morning" was on the same plateau as carrying the baby during the last three months of pregnancy.

Mom and I didn't want to sound ungrateful, but making coffee is one of the simpler things we do. To us, it's on the same domestic entry level as putting a grocery bag in the trash can or taking a frozen chicken out of the freezer to thaw.

Up until that moment, my dad had never done anything domestic before. "Making coffee in the morning" was something he could do without compromising his masculinity. He could still watch the Rams on Sunday and make coffee on Monday morning.

"Speaking of hanging it up," I said to my dad, "your grandson is thinking of retiring."

"From what? He's too young to retire."

"There is a precedent," I said. "Bjorn Borg stopped playing tennis when he was twenty-six, and I read the other day where Mary Lou Retton retired at eighteen."

"Eighteen!" he gasped.

"Hey, when you've appeared on the cover of *Time* magazine, written your autobiography, and skied with Dr. Ruth . . . what's left?"

"I don't understand kids today," he grumbled. "They just don't have the ambition we had to get ahead."

It was true. They never aspired to be a doctor because you had to wash above the elbows. Didn't want to be a priest because you had to work Sundays. And didn't want to be President of the United States because there was no chance for advancement. For awhile, one of them talked about being a game show contestant, but face it, he was too cheap to buy a vowel.

"Didn't he want to be a baseball player at one time?" asked Dad.

"Yeah, but that was only because you could grab up a handful of dirt, wipe it off on your pants, and spit in public. Don't worry, Dad, he'll find himself. Let me get you another cup of coffee from the kitchen." My dad gave a half smile.

The trouble with kids is they give 'em too much nowadays. They pay those kids for their old teeth, to go to bed, and to breathe!

Why doesn't anyone ever tell young people the truth about work? We have an entire generation of kids growing up who have been told that work must be "fun, relevant, and meaningful." The hell it is. It's discipline, competition, and repetition. So the paper route wasn't the religious experience they

*thought it would be. And the dirt and sweat from
the construction job didn't fulfill them? And they
didn't feel excitement selling velvet paintings of El-
vis door to door? That's because they're confusing
work with success. Success is fun, relevant, and
meaningful. Work is just plain dogging it. So why
do we do it?*

*Because those are the ethics that count for some-
thing, and if we don't maintain these things, we
lose something we desperately need to survive . . .
called dignity.*

"Dad, come quick!"

"What's the matter?" he shouted.

"I just came into the kitchen for more coffee and
I'm not alone," I said. "I saw a darting shadow
out of the corner of my eye."

My husband joined us. "What's the matter?"

"There's an animal in this kitchen . . . somewhere."

"What kind of an animal was it?" he snickered.
"Rocky Raccoon? The Flying Squirrel? Smokey
the Bear? How about Dumbo? Pogo? Charlie Tuna?
Name names."

"It was a disgusting mouse and stop talking like
he was wearing a letter sweater."

"What did it look like?" he asked.

"It was tall."

"It was probably just a baby that came in from
the garage."

This bit of wisdom from a man who told me last

year that a plague of crickets in my house was good luck and they ate two carpets.

Oh, I used to be naïve about animals. I wanted to believe they were male, unmarried, and traveling alone.

"Bill," I said, "I want you to go to the hardware store and get me fifteen traps, thirty-five boxes of painless death powder, eighteen aerosol insecticide sprays, five bottles of fast-acting mists, five plastic swatters, and a mallet."

"You have enough short-range missiles?" he asked, nudging my dad in the ribs and laughing.

My son joined us and said, "What's so funny?"

"Your mother is funny," said his granddad. "She's hysterical over a little mouse."

My son rushed over and grabbed the box by the toaster. "That was no mouse. That was my snake's dinner!"

Calmly, I walked from the kitchen to my bedroom where I shut the door, turned, and screamed.

"I WANT YOUR JOB, VANNA"

I love you, Jane Goodall. I really do.

I was filled with envy when you went to Africa in the sixties to observe the baboons and chimpanzees. I said, "Why not me, God? I could take the silence, the boredom, the isolation. Why was I chosen to stay behind to battle smog, bickering children, and aggressive leftovers?"

From time to time I would see you on a special on PBS, and for days afterward I would fantasize about climbing into a pair of shorts and a faded shirt, fastening my hair in a ponytail (where do you get all those rubber bands in a country without doorknobs?), and ascending to a solitary hill to write down what I saw.

No panty hose riding around your hips, no gas

gauge on empty, no need to shave your legs, no video games, no newspaper in the downspouts, no securing the house every night like Fort Knox . . . just blessed peace and only the need to worry about having a clean pair of shorts for the next day.

Sometimes, Jane, I'll go for months and not think too much about you, and then it's the weeks just before the holidays when I think about you a lot. I think about you when the kids are home and two of them are pounding out the first eight bars of "Heart and Soul" on the piano for three solid hours. I think about you when we run out of milk every six hours. I think of you when they invade my space with their smells and noises and possessions.

I think about you when a pregnant mouse escapes who was on a fertility drug and is expecting multiple births in my woodwork any minute. I'm a desperate woman, Jane, living in an atmosphere seen only in a bus station rest room.

I want your job!

I want to sit on a hillside and know that the phone won't ring the moment I sit down.

The more I watch my family, the more nonthreatening and civilized baboons seem. Obviously you have chosen the easy way out. I'll be all right in a few weeks. I always bounce back, but if I were you I'd look over my shoulder.

I want your job, Vanna White. What a breeze. You sleep late, go to the studio, go into makeup, and then for thirty minutes, watch people spin a

Wheel of Fortune. You don't have to do anything but smile and flip over vowels and consonants.

You don't have to fight traffic or defrost frozen hamburger in the dry cycle of the dishwasher or wear wet panty hose. You don't even have to make change when someone buys a vowel. Why couldn't I have fallen into something like that?

Charles Kuralt's job *On the Road* wouldn't be bad to take either. Ride along in an air-conditioned van, see a guy by the side of the road whittling famous presidents out of peanut shells, stop the van, and ''do'' twenty minutes. Call it a day and take off the next morning to find another subject.

Or maybe I'd like a job like hairdresser to Tina Turner, Grace Jones, and Cyndi Lauper. I could sit around and watch soaps and eat chocolate, and then once every six months they'd call for me and I'd whip out a can of spray paint or shellac and my job would be done for another six months.

I want your job, Lady Liberty. All you have to do is schlep around in a caftan, sporting upper arms that could fan Brazil, and looking like you've eaten every pigeon that came within arm's length.

You have a 35-foot waist, a 3-foot mouth, and an arm that holds seven tourists on a curved stairway, and no one says to you, ''Yes, but she's tall.''

But face it, I've got a job. A job that after thirty years leaves me unsure of myself, fraught with frustration, and no end in sight. I don't have the guts of Mayor Koch of New York to say, ''How am I doin'?''

Sometimes, I dare to look back and think about what I would have done differently. I always felt I should have been younger when the kids were born . . . about twelve or so. I'd have had more stamina and that's an age where everything is funny. The kids, in retrospect, should have been older. Maybe the bugs in their plumbing could have been worked out and they could communicate once in awhile.

I talked too much. I had good material, but I used it indiscriminately. Every hour I said, "Why don't you grow up?" and when they did, I accused them of wanting to be an adult too fast.

I never really looked at them. When I looked at their mouths, I saw dirt around them. When I looked at their noses, I saw them running. When I looked at their eyes, I saw them open when they should have been closed. When I saw their hair, it needed combing or cutting. I never really looked at the whole face without offering some advice.

For over twenty years, I invited myself into their lives. I put sweaters on them when I was cold, removed blankets from their beds when I was hot. I fed them when I was hungry and put them to bed when I was tired. I put them on diets when I was fat. I car-pooled them when I felt the distance was too far for me to walk. Then I told them they took a lot of my time.

I never realized as I dedicated my life to ring-

around-the-collar that cleanliness is not next to god-
liness . . . children are.

But oh Jane, Vanna, Charles, and Miss Liberty
. . . some days I'd kill for your jobs.

And this is one of them.

CAN WE TALK?

Saturday: 11 P.M.

paused at the door of the guest room to see what my daughter was watching on TV. On the small screen, a girl with a mouth like Emmett Kelly and electric hair rested her head on the chest of a man sleeping next to her. She traced circular 8's in the hair on his chest. He awakened and kissed her.

"I love you," she whispered, "but I know so little about you."

"What do you want to know?" he breathed.

"What's your last name?"

"Chernowsky."

"Is that Polish?" she asked brightly.

It was the usual story of instant sex . . . just add a bed and stir. "Don't people get married anymore?" I asked.

"Not if you want to keep your ratings," she said.

"Are you saying that marriage can't pull a 30 share on TV? That a couple can't hold something together for thirteen weeks without being canceled?"

"I'm saying marriage isn't particularly dramatic, intoxicating, passionate, or riveting."

"I suppose your father and I are just hanging on for the social security checks."

"Mother, I do not want to have this conversation again."

"I just want to know why the resistance to marriage."

"There is more to life than washing socks and snapping beans," she said. "Women have to know who they are and have a job that's fulfilling before they settle down. God, even Barbie's gone corporate!"

"Barbie as in Ken, two-inch bust, who never has to worry about hair color, who just removes her head?"

"That's the one," she said, flipping off the TV set. "It's not easy for a forty-eight-year-old woman to enter the job market."

"Barbie is forty-eight years old!"

"With no thoughts of getting married. Don't look so shocked, Mother, what did you think she and Ken were doing in that cardboard car under the bed . . . playing John Denver records?"

"Not Barbie."

"If you took the rubber band off her hair, her face would fall to her knees."

"There's no need to be cruel. I've never asked a lot of my children. Just that they get married and make me a mother-in-law and a grandmother . . . in that order."

"You wouldn't like it," she said. "I hear being a mother-in-law is overrated. Trust me, she rides to the church in the front seat with her son and rides home in another car. She's in the front row at the wedding and in the kitchen at the reception."

"I don't believe it."

"And the only time she gets the grandchild is when it is contagious or they can't get a regular sitter. Besides, it isn't easy anymore finding someone to get married to."

"Then you have thought about it."

"Not really. Only that in 1955, 2,073,719 boy babies were born. Out of that number, 872,638 died in the war, in accidents or of natural causes, leaving 1,201,081. You still with me?" I nodded. "Since 10 percent get married and 5 percent get divorced, you can assume 15 percent of this total are marrying and divorcing one another, leaving 1,020,919. Homosexuals represent possibly 10 percent, bringing the eligibles down to 918,827. Of the little less than a million eligibles roaming around, 5 percent don't know their sign and don't even care. Another 5 percent are tied to their mothers by a food fixation. That leaves only 20 percent who are searching for a girl who will pick up their clothes, run their baths, burn her fingers shelling their three-minute eggs, run their errands, bear them a child every year, look like a fashion model, tend their needs when they are sick, and hold down a full-time job outside the home to make payments on their boat. Besides, Grandma has already been on my case. She said all I need is a nice personality and a sense of humor and they'll be standing in line at my front door.''

I couldn't believe Grandma was using that old chestnut on her granddaughter. She told me that too. I'm no dummy. When I was in school, I saw boys date girls with the personality of a leftover, but if she was stacked, she could get a date to take her to have her teeth cleaned.

Personality and sense of humor got to be a joke . . . then it got to be a stigma. Every time someone was trying to palm off a girl who breathed through her mouth and had a nice tooth, they'd say, ''She has a great personality.'' Or when they were trying to set you up with a boy who raised earthworms and had a collection of Spanish dolls on his bed, they'd say, ''He has a wonderful sense of humor.''

''Forget about Grandma and her personality and sense of humor,'' I said. ''You should be looking for a man who manufactures batteries.''

''I thought you wanted me to marry a doctor.''

''Marry a man who turns out batteries for a living and those rosebud lips of yours will never touch plastic again.''

"Oh please."

"I'm telling you we've gone from the Stone Age to the Battery Age. You put four to six to eight batteries these days in everything from talking robots to electronic games to your toothbrush. Christmas cards run on batteries, so do home computers and cameras and dolls. No one wants anything anymore that sits there and does nothing."

"You have just described three-fourths of the marriages in this country."

"We're back to that," I said. "If you ask me, you're looking in all the wrong places. You're looking in bars and health clubs. Forget the bars. Everyone's happy in a bar and you can't trust health clubs. Everyone holds his stomach in. There is an alternative to the bar scene."

"Which is?" she said suspiciously.

"The supermarket. I saw it on television. 'Singles Night' for men and women who want to meet people in a natural setting."

"What's natural about squeezing the same avocado?"

"It sounds great. You just get a little name tag at the door, and the first couple to exchange phone numbers gets a free dinner someplace and then you play games."

"What kind of games?"

"I don't know. Someone said they had bowling contests with toilet paper."

"Be still my beating heart," she said. "I'll bet every five minutes, the PA announces, 'Attention

Shoppers. A real bargain on cupcakes this week. Mid-twenties, single, great shelf-life, check her out on aisle 3.' ''

"Why do you make everything sound so sexist?" I asked.

"Because it is. Somehow I can't see myself reaching for the same brand of wheat germ at the same time as the man of my dreams."

"Are you still seeing that man you brought by last month?"

"He was shallow, insensitive, crude, chauvinistic, married, and bragged about setting fires."

"So give him a chance. What about the other one who loved Barry Manilow?"

"He thought ERA stood for Earned Run Averages."

"And the accountant who lived at home with his mother?"

"He thought ERA stood for a detergent."

"Didn't your brother fix you up with a nice boy?"

"My brother's idea of nice boy came by in a pickup truck with a bumper sticker on it that said THIS MAY NOT BE THE MAYFLOWER, BUT YOUR DAUGHTER JUST CAME ACROSS IN IT."

"That's a strange metaphor."

"Mother, let's get down to the core of this conversation. Who just had another grandchild?"

"Mayva."

"I knew it."

The last thing I want is to hand down guilt to my

children. I have never wanted to infringe on their personal lives or become a burden, but I just have difficulty in understanding why they want me to die from a broken heart leaving no grandchildren.

What am I asking? A small wedding, a few months to adjust, a full-term pregnancy, and then twenty years or so out of their lives to raise my grandchild. Is that expecting too much?

How am I supposed to feel when all of my contemporaries are whipping out billfolds containing sixty-five candid pictures of grandchildren and I'm still carrying around June Allyson and Dick Powell?

It isn't bad enough that I have to tromp through miles of toys at Christmas with these women and listen to how their little angels threw their arms around Grandma's neck and said, "I wub you mamaw." I have to be reminded if my kids don't get off the dime—and soon—I will be the only grandmother who cannot feed herself.

Why are they putting off having a family? Could it be that we have frightened them with our perfection? Our imperfection? No, it's probably our perfection.

Maybe they figure they can't measure up to taking a birthday cake hot from the oven at 11:24 at night and stuffing it into a yawning mouth saying, "Eat! In thirty-six minutes, it won't be your birthday anymore."

Maybe they can't face up to washing the dog in tomato juice when he encounters a skunk, sitting through a concert of battling French horns, or knocking out a wall in the dead of winter to make room for a ping-pong table that will be used only to throw books on after school.

I don't like to . . . excuse the expression . . . labor the issue, but in a few years I will be too old to be a grandmother. After all, there are certain duties that come with a grandchild. Timing is everything.

In a few years I will not have the strength to crawl around on the floor and play, baby-sit longer than two hours, or remember all the wisdom that made me such a wonderful mother.

"There's no reason in this world why my children shouldn't be miserable and tied down like the rest of us," I blurted out.

My daughter shook her head and smiled. "That's it, isn't it?"

"I was only kidding."

"Remember when we were kids and visited a home where there were velvet drapes, glass coffee tables, and white bathroom towels, and you always said, 'Why not? They don't have kids.' "

"I didn't mean . . ."

"When we turned the dining room into a fort to play and the place was a mess, you always came in and said, 'This house will never look like anything as long as I have kids.' And I remember that day when we were on a bus riding into town and a really neat car with a woman in a yellow chiffon scarf pulled up next to us. I looked at you, Mom, and I didn't have to be told how much you envied her. I could see it. I know you never thought we listened to anything you said, but I heard you that day . . . loud and clear.''

She listened . . . but what did she hear?

Did she hear my tears the day she was born? What a pity because never, before or since, had I known such joy. For awhile, I couldn't even speak to anyone about it. I just played with her fingers and tried to memorize every feature of her face to savor the moment.

Did she hear my prayers the night of her asthma attack and I was threatened with the loss of something I could not bear to even think of living without?

Did she hear what was in my heart when she graduated and I sat in the darkness with tears in my eyes?

Did she hear my smugness the day on the bus when we looked at the woman in the new car? I was saying to myself, ''Lady, I wouldn't trade you even for what I've got.''

She listened. But some emotions don't make a lot of noise. It's hard to hear pride. Caring is real faint—like a heartbeat. And pure love—why, some days it's so quiet, you don't even know it's there.

She looked at me and said, ''Don't worry. I'll manage.''

I said, ''Kids! They make you crazy.''

I could have bitten my tongue in half.

ARE WE TALKING MEANINGFUL YET?

In the media room, through the miracle of VCR, my son was lying prone on the sofa watching *Miami Vice*.

I perched on the arm of a chair and listened.

"If you chill out, those low-life slime buckets will sew your fingers to the inside of your mouth. I'm telling you those maggots are lookin' for a big score at Cokeland, and if Customs doesn't like you, you're gonna get bake and shake. That means you're looking at a dime and a half mandatory, so if the deal's goin' down, play ball or do the time and let us in on the sweep. If it's White Christmas, you're dead meat anyway."

I turned to my son. "Why do I have the idea

that they're not talking about Bing Crosby and Rosemary Clooney?''

''Hey, I don't have to watch this now. I can save it until tomorrow,'' he said, flipping it to another channel.

''No wonder we can't communicate,'' I said. ''We don't even speak the same language.''

''You've been saying that for years,'' he said.

''It's true. I don't understand cop shows and I've never been able to understand what those people said on those records you played when you were home, but I'm sure it has to do with sex, violence, drugs, or Satanism.''

''What album is that and who is the artist?'' he said showing some excitement.

''All of them. Of course, all I heard was oh, oh and be be and gimee and I won you, but you probably heard more.''

''I have a confession, Mom,'' he said. ''That's all I ever heard. If there was more to it, I couldn't understand 'em either.''

I didn't believe him for a moment. We're talking about a kid who watched a Michael Jackson video so many times he could predict the exact second his ears grew fur . . . the same kid who kept a cockroach as a pet because he couldn't bear to kill it and yet watched six hours of graves being dug. He found entertainment in someone swinging from a guillotine, cars exploding, and a child eating an ice cream cone in an electric chair on MTV.

Something strange was moving on the TV set. "What's that?" I asked.

"It's called a Cyndi Lauper."

"What happened to her hair? It looks like she slept on the same side so long she went bald."

"She has it cut that way."

"Is this a telethon to help her?"

"Mom! It's her new video. She's great."

"Greater than Marge Fexter's niece who is visiting and would like you to take her to a movie?"

"I told you. I don't go out with anyone with a button-down oxford cloth blouse. That's gross."

"You're just like your father. I can't communicate with him either."

It's true. Men take forever to get to the point. Not me. When he walks into the house, I say right off, "Why do you want me dead?" and he knows right up front that he has set the thermostat back too far and it's so cold I'm afraid to fall asleep.

Like his sons, he answers every question with a question.

If I say, "How do you like my dress?" he answers, "Are they wearing that style this year?"

"How do you like my haircut?"

"Are you pleased with it?"

"What time do you want to go to dinner?"

"What time do you want to eat?"

Our vocabulary is different. When women ask, "What do you think of this casserole?" "interesting" is not the reaction we are looking for.

It makes me furious when men carry on an intensive conversation with a phantom voice for twenty minutes, responding with, "No! I don't believe it. What kind of numbers are we talking about? Wiped out, huh? How could this have happened? Keep me posted. Call me in the middle of the night if you have to." And when he hangs up and you ask, "What was that all about?" he says, "Nothing."

The TV once again grabbed my attention. I saw a singer who turned into a bumblebee and flew in pursuit of a girl. He appeared in her bath disguised as a piece of soap. He appeared in her hairbrush and in her medicine chest. He appeared as a bug crawling under the blanket. He scaled the Empire State Building, and from time to time his head left his body.

My son looked at me. "Now don't tell me you don't understand that!"

"I hope you won't take this the wrong way," I said, "but I think you're very sick."

"Mom, parents and their kids aren't supposed to communicate. It breaks down the hostility that we need to sustain our relationship. Remember how you and Dad were always on my case about my long hair?"

"We may have mentioned it a few times."

"Mom! Every time you were supposed to give me the kiss of peace during Mass, you'd turn to me and say, 'Get a haircut, Weirdo.'"

"Look, I didn't go through thirty-six hours of

labor to give birth to Sandra Dee," I said. "And that disgusting beard."

"Everyone had a beard: Merlin the Magician, Doc of the Seven Dwarfs . . . Santa Claus."

"None of them had a mother," I challenged.

"The point is," he said, "do you remember what happened when I got my hair cut and shaved off my beard?"

I remembered. We became strangers. Our relationship had always been built on a firm ground of criticism. His long hair and his beard brought us together. From the moment he entered the door until the moment he left, we had rapport . . . feelings . . . threats . . . and untold guilt.

I found myself planning our next encounter and thinking up creative ways to bring up the subject of his hair. I used to flash a picture of Dick Clark and say, "Now there's a boy who enjoys rock 'n' roll and you can still see his ears."

Once on a vacation, it was all we talked about from Gary, Indiana, to Salt Lake City, Utah. It really made the time fly.

And then one night he came in and his hair was cut short and his beard was gone. We had nothing to say to one another. Nothing to nag about. Nothing to criticize. Nothing to communicate. Finally, his father said, "So, why didn't you tell us you were getting your hair cut?" We chewed on it for the rest of the evening. It was like old times.

Maybe he was right. Maybe parents didn't try

hard enough to communicate with kids in their ver-
nacular. I couldn't just come right out and ask him
when he was going to find work, so I tried speaking his language.

"So, how are you coming at mainstreaming your
talents?"

"Do you have a problem with that?" he
asked.

"I thought there was something we could
share."

"There was an ad for a pizza delivery boy, but
it wasn't meaningful."

I smiled. "Fulfillment without gratification is
just the tip of the iceberg."

"Boy, isn't that the truth," he said. "Choices.
That's what life is all about."

"Have you tried networking?" I asked.

"Negative. There's no real esteem there, you
know what I mean?"

"I know exactly," I nodded. "Pressure without
upward mobility is just another meaningless expression of verbal skills."

"You really do understand, don't you?" he
said.

"I have always said challenge without inade-
quacy is the social glue that holds us all together."

He smiled and looked at me. "Boy, Mom, I
never dreamed you knew how I felt. If we had had
this dialogue ten years ago, maybe we would have

had a better relationship with one another. I'm going to try what you said.''

I said good night.

God, I'd have given anything to know what I said.

GOOD NIGHT . . .
WHOEVER YOU ARE . . .

I stopped by the bathroom and heard the water running and my son humming.

"Are you home?" I shouted, rapping on the door.

"What do you think?"

"Do you have towels?"

"Don't I always?"

"Did you lock the back door?"

"Was it unlocked?"

"What time do you leave tomorrow?"

"Do you have to know tonight?"

"You want to sleep in?"

"What kind of a question is that?"

"Good night!"

It was wonderful to know I could still communicate with my kids.

"SAY GOOD NIGHT, GRACIE"

Saturday: 11:30 P.M.

My husband was propped up in bed reading the paper when I closed the door softly.

"Where have you been?"

"Talking to the kids," I said.

"So, how's everything with them?"

"Ask them yourself."

"You're still sore about the mouse, aren't you?"

"I'm not sore about the mouse."

"Your father and I both agreed you were overreacting when you called the Realtor and demanded she list the house immediately."

"I said I was sorry, so let's forget it. Are all the cars in and the lights out?"

"Ummm. I hope the picture for the Christmas

card turns out. Speaking of Christmas, you haven't told me what you want this year.''

''Do I have to tell you? If you really knew me, you wouldn't have to ask,'' I said.

''What a thing to say,'' he said. ''Of course I know you. I know you're practical, no-nonsense, and like things for the house that you wouldn't buy yourself.''

In all these years, he never knew how I stood in front of a Mr. Fredericks window and lusted. You'd think he knew I always wanted the ultimate nightgown that you had to dry clean . . . a gown so filmy that when the doorbell rang or one of the kids came into the room, you had to throw a coat or an afghan over yourself to avoid arrest. It would have enough fur around the bottom to put in fur storage for safekeeping.

I always wanted a jumpsuit made out of fake animal, preferably leopard or cheetah, and fake fingernails so long I couldn't make meat loaf without losing half the hamburger under my nails.

I always wanted a pair of eight-inch-heel bedroom slippers that killed your feet but made your ankles look tiny . . . slippers so impractical that the only thing they were good for was dangling from your toe or drinking champagne out of.

I'll get a vegetable steamer. I know it.

''What about you?'' I asked. ''What do you want?''

''Oh, you know me,'' he said, ''I just like to sit

around and watch everyone else open up their gifts. I don't need anything . . . really.''

The reason he doesn't need anything . . . really! . . . is because every year, three days before Christmas, he buys everything for himself. Last year he brought home packages containing underwear, stacks of shorts, shirts, and socks. As the blood drained away from my face, he displayed a sweater to kick around in, bedroom slippers to replace the ones that had fallen apart, and a money clip that struck his fancy.

I still had my ace in the hole: a bathrobe which he needed desperately. He showed me a wristband to hold his car keys and change when he jogged, a book on fishing lures he had seen advertised, and some great gloves for skiing. The bathrobe he bought was being monogrammed.

"You know what you really need is some help around here," he said. "What if I got you a housekeeper to help around the holidays?"

"You're too kind," I said, "but I still haven't gotten over Mrs. Rutledge."

"I remember it was an unpleasant experience, but I honestly never saw the woman."

I never saw the woman either. We communicated by notes on the refrigerator. They were usually a day apart.

The first day on the job she wrote, "Mrs. Bombeck: There is a dog's mess at the end of the sofa.'' Signed, Wilma.

The next morning I left her a note: ''Wilma, I know.'' Signed, Mrs. Bombeck.

The following day: ''Mrs. Bombeck, what do you want me to do with it?'' Signed, Wilma.

A reply was posted the next day: ''Wilma, you are limited on options. You can surround it with sand and use it as a putting green, gift-wrap it and amaze your friends, or clean it up. I prefer the latter.'' Signed, Mrs. Bombeck.

The next day she wrote, ''Mrs. Bombeck: I was going to clean up the you-know-what, but the sweeper smells funny and sounds strange and won't pick up anything. Can you fix it?'' Signed, Wilma.

The next morning, a new note from Wilma said, ''The sweeper works fine. What did you do to it?''

I wrote a note the following day. ''Wilma: I emptied the sweeper bag.'' Mrs. Bombeck.

Several weeks passed before a new note appeared. ''Mrs. Bombeck: You know that little problem I told you about two weeks ago. I think I solved it. I moved the sofa over it and you can hardly notice it now.'' Signed, Wilma.

The note the next morning was short: ''Wilma, you're fired.'' Signed, Mrs. Bombeck.

Wilma's last epistle appeared the next morning. ''Mrs. Bombeck: There is another dog mess I didn't tell you about. It's hard to find. I'm the only one who knows where it is. Good-bye.'' Signed, Wilma.

"Our kids think we have everything," I said, turning off the bathroom light.

"Is that why we get cats in tennis shoes and a kangaroo with string coming out of its navel?"

"They're probably right. We do have everything. At this stage, having them spend a Saturday night with you is worth a gift certificate on the Orient Express."

"They try," he said, flipping off the light by his bed.

Try! They go through life trying to please us . . . looking for approval . . . trying to fit into the family puzzle. Sometimes we forget how hard it is to be a child.

In the darkness I reflected on the weekend and drifted to sleep. As I slept, I dreamt that the roles were reversed. My children were the parents . . . and I was the child.

It was terrible standing down there wedged among all those knees. I couldn't get a drink of water, mail a letter, or open a door. Cars were worse. If I didn't kill myself getting a window, I just sat there on the seat with my legs sticking straight out, staring at the back of the seat. Every once in awhile, one of the kids would shout, "You know I can't drive and shout at you at the same time," but that wasn't true at all.

At the supermarket, I was just standing there when without warning, someone whipped me off the floor and forced my legs through a grocery seat that was so cold my teeth frosted up.

I never got introduced. Sometimes someone would say, "Oh, is this the holy terror you were telling me about?" but for all purposes, I had no name.

I took naps when I wasn't sleepy, ate when I wasn't hungry, had sweaters put on me when I wasn't cold, and got thrown into swimming pools when I didn't want to swim.

I was tossed into the air when I had an upset stomach, forced to go to the bathroom whether I had to go or not, and ordered to stop crying when I had a perfectly good reason for doing it.

Sometimes my kids laughed and when I asked what they were laughing about, they said, "We'll tell you when you're older."

I never did anything right. I played with chewing gum, wiped my hands off on my dress, leaned back on chairs, made faces in the toaster, and sniffed instead of using a handkerchief. Once when I came into the kitchen with a comb in my hand, I thought life was all over.

The worst was when we went to a house of my children's friends. They said, "Look, Mom, would you and Dad stop dawdling or we're going to be late at Debbie's and Mike's house. And I'm telling you both before we go, we don't want you whining about when we are coming home and running in and out every two minutes to 'tell.' And for crying out loud, take something to do—some of your favorite toys. Mom, why don't you take your needlepoint? That would keep you occupied for awhile.

Your home workshop is out of the question, Dad. It's too big. Take something small . . . like maybe your key ring to play with.''

At the house, introductions were brief. ''This is my mom and dad, but you'll forget their names anyway. Say hello. And would you look at your parents! I swear they've grown a foot since we last saw them. How are things at work? And where did you get that pretty dress? I want you to meet my parents. Mom is forty-seven and Dad is forty-eight. You should have a lot in common. Now run along and get acquainted. Maybe their mom will show you her new microwave oven and their dad his new power mower. Keep it down now. We want to talk.''

Later, as the children were really having a good time, the four of us approached them. ''Kids, can we go home now? All of us are sleepy. Besides, Dad has some figures to pull together before work tomorrow morning.''

The kids looked at one another. ''Isn't that just like parents. Putting everything off until the last minute. I swear you can't take them anywhere and have a good time. What do you say we get together soon without the A-D-U-L-T-S?''

On the way home the kids said, ''I love Debbie and Mike, but their parents are really spoiled. I hope you two didn't drink a lot of liquids or you'll be up all night. And don't you dare fall asleep on the way home or we'll leave you in the car all night.''

I sat up in bed with a start.

"Bad dream?" yawned my husband.

"Keep it down," I said sleepily. "We're supposed to be asleep."

"RUNNING AWAY FROM HOME"

Sunday: 9:20 A.M.

I heard the voices all the way to the back of the house. My daughter was accusing her brother of taking her Jockey underwear out of the dryer, and he was accusing her of not returning his hair dryer. It wasn't a conversation you'd want to put into a time capsule.

I hated mornings. The only way I survived them when they were children was through self-hypnosis. I always thought if the good Lord had wanted me to speak in the mornings, He'd have put a recording in my chest and a string in the back of my neck. I had a basic morning vocabulary of seventeen words: "No. I don't care. It's in the dirty clothes hamper. Mustard or ketchup? In your father's billfold.''

That was it. There were no additions or subtractions in two decades. Mornings were unbearable because not one of the kids had an ounce of organization in his life. They always sat at the breakfast table with a pencil poised over a blank sheet of paper at 8 A.M. and asked, ''Now tell me all you know about the Egyptian rulers of the fifth century because if Miss Shorhamm doesn't get a fifteen-page report by 10 A.M., she is going to keep me in the sophomore class for the rest of my life.''

Or they would come dragging out with a piece of blank paper and a pencil and demand a note to get back into class using the Latin word for diarrhea to avoid humiliation.

There was the matter of getting dressed. Somewhere there is an unwritten law that a child will wear to school (a) only what is in the dirty clothes hamper, (b) what needs ironing, (c) what he is forbidden ever to leave the house wearing, (d) what everyone else is wearing (c and d are often the same thing).

No one will ever know the conversations that took place between 7 and 7:30 in the morning.

''Mom, have you seen my navy sweater?''

''The one with the buttons missing and the hole in the shoulder?''

''That's it. They're taking class pictures today.''

It didn't get any better when they got older. They never anticipated anything. They never considered that it might turn cold or that a rain might come up and they would need an umbrella or a coat. They never figured a bank would cash their check on the same day it was received. Time held no limitations for them. They came to me with straight faces the third week of August and said, "Hey, you going near the post office today or tomorrow? I want to get my application in for a college this fall."

They never figured an airplane would leave on time. Even if they were somewhere on the freeway at the scheduled time of departure, they figured they were in great shape.

"Incidentally," I yelled to the two who were now snapping at a Danish in mid-air, "What time does your brother's plane leave?"

"Around 10," said my daughter. "Don't worry. We'll get him there and then we've both got to buzz off."

"It's 9:20 now!" I said. "Where is he?"

"He's in the shower."

"He was in the shower last night when I went to bed."

"Make your point," said my son.

"Here comes the wethead now," said my daughter.

"Your plane is at 10," I said. "I'll get your father. He'll want to say good-bye."

He grabbed a carton of milk out of the refrigerator and began drinking from it. "Mom, take it easy. You're going to have a heart attack. Do you have a bigger suitcase? I'm going to take some records to the coast.''

His brother volunteered to put it together and left the room.

"How long does it take to do laundry?'' he asked.

"My God! You're talking crazy now.''

"I gotta call this guy for an address.'' He dialed and I stood at his elbow the entire time with all the hysteria of Butterfly McQueen about to deliver Melanie's baby.

When he hung up, he said, "Let me write down a place for you to go to buy a new mouse for the snake. When he gets hungry, he strikes at you.''

I thought I was going to be sick.

"What time is it now?'' he asked.

I blinked.

"That's right. All the clocks blink around here. Hey, guys, let's do it. Love you Mom. See you Thanksgiving. Is Dad around? I wanta say good-bye . . . tell him I'll call.''

The other two exchanged hugs and good-byes and piled into the car.

My husband arrived at the door just as they all pulled out of the driveway. "It was wonderful having him home. He looks a little taller, doesn't he?''

"Possibly,'' I said. "I guess he talked to you a lot about what he's doing? He'd talk to his father about that, wouldn't he?''

"Did it seem to you he had a handle on things? He would talk to his mother about that.''

"I suppose so," I said, "but if he had anything definite on his mind, he'd ask your advice, wouldn't he?"

Neither of us said anything for awhile. Then his dad said, "I'll tell you the truth. I never set eyes on the kid the entire three days he was home."

"I never saw him either," I said.

"I sorta got a glimpse of him the night he split when we were showing our slides of the Smoky Mountains, but not enough to tell anything. He was here, wasn't he?"

"What a silly thing to say. Of course he was here. I talked with him several times through the bathroom door."

"Wait a minute," said my husband. "Does he have a gray sweater with three stripes on the sleeve? I think I saw him one night holding both refrigerator doors wide open like he was a Welcome Wagon lady."

"That wasn't our son. That was his friend David."

"I wish I'd known that. I apologized to him for not spending more time with him. I'll say this. He's different, all right."

Raising kids was like playing poker with strangers. You never knew if you had a bluffer, one with a killer instinct, or one who changed rules in the middle of the game.

I think I was terrified of them from the moment they were born. I never trusted one of them with a mouthful of strained peas. Even after I stopped pinching their lips together and watching them swallow, I was afraid to take my eyes off them lest I get it all back in my face.

I had children who were eaters. They ate everything: chairs, turtles, blankets, hymnals, shoes, and anything else that didn't fight back. I never slept behind a door that wasn't locked.

I watched my son play tennis at a nice club one day wearing his pajama top and cutoff jeans with boxer shorts hanging out of the legs. I was horrified he signed up for the court under his right name.

"He always seemed to stand around like he had a lip full of Novocain," said my husband. "Did he ever talk to you?"

"One day when I was baking a cake, I broke an egg and it slid down the side of the bowl and the entire length of the cupboard and onto the floor. He said, 'Way to go, Mom.' "

"That was it?"

"No, there was the brief period when he first went away to school. Remember, he used to call us about every fifteen minutes?"

"I remember. That's when it cost $2.40 for the first three minutes. What did he talk about?"

"We paid $3.10 to hear him inquire if we had any mail for him from *Reader's Digest* Sweepstakes . . . $4.70 to find out if it was raining where we are . . . $6.34 to inquire if the dog missed him . . . and $3.04 to find out how often you can take a twelve-hour cold capsule."

"God knows I tried," said his father. "One day I picked him up at school and when he got out, I noticed a picture on the floor of the back seat done in crayon. I had it framed and I took him to my office and there among the degrees, honors, and plaques for membership was his simple little picture, remember? And I said, 'What do you think of that?' He said, 'It's nice, but why would you want Freddie Cohen's picture of his family hanging in your office?' "

There was no doubt about it . . . this one, racing to catch an airplane that was at the end of the runway when he left home, defied all books on childraising . . . all the timetables for development . . . all the clichés that worked for mothers from the beginning of time.

I remember when he was late for dinner one night and I said, "What's the matter? Get hit by a truck?" A truck had run a red light and it nipped the back of his bicycle and threw him for a few bruises.

And there was my Mother's Day speech of 1978. It was one of the most eloquent speeches of sacrifice and dedication ever delivered to a group of ungrateful bums who appeared presentless. As I was getting to the good stuff about how the doctor had always said I was too short for pregnancy and would never wear pleated skirts again, and how all they ever thought about was themselves, the doorbell rang and a large bouquet of flowers was delivered with Mother's Day greetings from the three of them.

You'd have thought that I would have learned my lesson, but he was off one year in another country working when I wrote him a searing letter ending with, "Why haven't you written? Is your arm broken?"

He wrote back it was just his wrist. I should have known better.

ALONE AT LAST

Sunday: 9:35 A.M.

"Move your feet," I said to my husband as I shoved a broom under them.

He put down his coffee cup and continued reading the paper at the breakfast room table. "Good Lord," he said, "remember the restaurant we went to with Dick and Bernice? You know, the one with Brick, Wendy, Stud, and Frank?" I nodded. "Well, it seems they've been cited for violations of sanitation procedures. Listen to this:

" 'Food not covered in refrigerator, improper dishwashing practices, carbon buildup on pans, corroded vent fan, raw garbage in garbage cans in kitchen, no soap or towels at sink, evidence of rodents on premises.' "

I looked at him tiredly. "Add rancid butter dish

by phone and a hair dryer on the countertop and you've just described this breakfast room.''

''It's not that bad,'' he said.

''This place is a dump! Trust me when I tell you the trash flow is at flood stage. I'm going to make some tracks in it today.''

''Tell me you're not going to play musical furniture again.''

''I am not going to play musical furniture. I just bought a few new pillows to brighten the place up.''

''Thank God.''

''I just want the sofa bed brought out of the den because it matches the pillows, so the living room sofa will be returned to the media room and the two chairs to the bedroom suite. The picture grouping over the sofa goes into the hallway so the bookcases will have to go on the opposite wall which will, of course, necessitate moving the TV set and the antenna. And I want to make some changes in the personal fitness room.''

''Why don't we just have it condemned and boarded up?''

''The spa isn't working out in there.''

''You mean the scale and the exercise bicycle. Where are you going to put it now?''

I honestly didn't know. The exercise bicycle, which seemed like such a good idea at the time, had been everywhere from the media room where I could watch TV and pedal my way to Linda Evans to the breakfast room where it clashed with the dishes.

For awhile I had it in the closet in our bedroom suite, but it was such a hassle lugging it out from behind the skis and the card table, I put it in the bathroom.

"We could put it in the sun room," I said hopefully.

"The sun room is only a sun room when the sun is shining. Right now, it's still the porch and it has no heat. That would eliminate your using the bicycle in the winter months."

"I want to cry," I said holding his gaze. "Now, where would you like your chair?"

"I like it where it is."

"It can't stay. It won't match the sofa bed and the new pillows."

I knew I was skating on thin ice. This chair was his throne. All decrees came from it. "Keep those kids quiet." "Get me a cold one while you're up." "Did you lock the doors?" "Tell them I'll call them back."

I learned the importance of a man's chair early in life. I learned that he may love several wives, embrace several cars, be true to more than one political philosophy, and be equally committed to several careers, but he will have only one comfortable chair in his life.

I learned it will be an ugly chair.

It will match nothing in the entire house.

It will never wear out.

I had tried them all. The canvas butterfly chair in shocking pink that he used to sink into and whimper, "I'm ready to get out of the chair now. Can someone come and get me?"

There was the antique chair Grandma left me where he had no place to put his tackle box and flies when he sorted them. The wooden rocker, the beanbags, contours, ottomans, headrests, loose cushions, plastic, bucket seat, tufted arms, Queen Anne, early attic, Victorian . . . all became history.

This chair was a bilious green recliner that elevated his feet and flattened out his shoulders. If it had a Water Pik on it, it would have looked like a dental chair.

From September through January during the football season, it was his home. I used to worry about him. It couldn't be good for him sitting there day in and day out nearly comatose watching plays, instant replays, stop action, pregame and postgame interviews, and wrap-ups.

I read where a bartender who watched three games nonstop on New Year's Day developed sharp chest pains and shortness of breath afterwards. He was diagnosed as too much inactivity.

When you think about it, it made a lot of sense. Most men just aren't in shape to relax that much . . . especially after a long summer of watching a few tennis matches and an occasional golf tournament. I always thought there should be a few aerobic exercises for football couch potatoes.

Like the warm-up: Stand in the middle of the floor, turn your neck to the right, all the way to where the screens need to be replaced by storm windows before October. Now pivot your neck to the left far enough to see the burned-out porch light and the trees that need fertilizing.

Next, try to touch the floor, which needs sanding, with your fingers. And finally, stretch and reach, extending your waist all the way over to where the pipes are leaking under the sink.

Now, for the arms, grab a stack of papers from the top of the basement stairs and, balancing them, make small circles as you head toward the garage. Make it burn. While you're in the garage, work the shoulder muscles by heaving some of that insulation that has been sitting around for three years in the attic.

Ready for aerobics? Start slowly, running in place, then run past the bathroom where the toilet needs to be reseated, the bedroom that needs painting, and through the front door where the bell no longer works. Eight minutes should increase your heart rate.

For the cool-down, sit on the floor with legs outstretched and bend over one knee. You should be at eye level with your wife who is painting the baseboards. Next, lie on your back and tighten every muscle in your body: the buttocks, the pelvis, the arms, and the legs. Now, relax. Clear your mind of the dog that wants to be let out, the phone ringing off the hook, and the timer on the oven.

"You are not getting rid of my chair," he said emphatically.

"Okay, but it will have to go in the guest room. And you'll have to wear something beige with it."

"Why are you acting like a crazy person today?" he asked. "It's Sunday, so just sit down and enjoy the peacefulness while you have it."

He didn't understand.

In the last three days, I had met my past. My life before deadlines, travels, and career. Before I became a fulfilled woman of the eighties, before my worth was measured by a credit line and a gold card . . . before I got my black belt in goal-setting.

The clock said it was 12 and blinking. In my other life, it would have given the correct time of the morning and I would have three kids who smelled of spray starch and vitamins off to school with lunch boxes and thermoses of soup they wouldn't bother to open.

I would promise myself that I would knit until 10 and then absolutely get dressed and bring the house up to minimal standards.

Then I would remove spots, add water, scrub toilets, write letters, kill roaches, polish shoes, clean ears, plant trees, mend wading pools, and blow up balloons.

I would hustle food, keep laundry moving, do volunteer work, decorate the house, keep staples in supply, counsel, discipline, mediate arguments, hand down decisions, and listen. I would listen a lot.

I would call my mother "just to talk," check in with my best friend to see if she too had lost control of her body, and visit with the neighbors and complain about the trash pickup.

Later, I would fry chicken, bake biscuits, and whip up something fattening for dinner.

I bedded the kids down between clean sheets and reveled in a day without a call from school or a call to the doctor. It was my turf.

I could hardly wait to leave the "crud detail" as I called it. I wanted to go to a place where you were important and people listened to what you had to say. Mothering hadn't done that . . . and yet . . . wouldn't it be ironic if my turf yielded the most important commodity being grown today? A family? A crop of children, seeded by two people, nourished by love, watered by tears, and in eighteen or twenty years harvested into worthwhile human beings to go through the process again. What if nothing else I would do would equal it in importance? Wouldn't you have thought someone would have told me?

I looked at my husband reading his paper, oblivious that our past, present, and future were at this moment speeding away from our lives at a frightening pace. They expect him to feel as strongly as I. Fathers were different than Mothers.

"Look," I said, "just sit there and read your paper and I'll go upstairs and move a few things around in the guest room. I'll call you when I'm ready for the chair.''

I know she will. God, it's quiet.

She thinks the Empty Nest is a feminine condition . . . a bored, depressed, neurotic woman peeking through starched lace curtains, holding a plate of freshly baked brownies, and eagerly awaiting the arrival of her son's laundry.

She never sees a father, ridden with guilt and regrets for all the time he was "busy" and, when they finally came home, argues about that stupid car!

I told myself it was going to be different this time. God was giving me a second chance. I was going to be there for them. How could I? They kept hours like hamsters. When I was asleep, they were up. When they were awake, they were on the phone. I spent thirty minutes talking to a son behind a closed door about how he felt about life, only to have him yell out, "I'm for it."

I envy these new fathers of the eighties. They're allowed to cry, to sweat, and to fail. Not me. I was raised to have a garage full of tools that I hated, talk car mileage, and bear the burden of being the sole breadwinner. I was the threat—the one they waited until he got home to get what they deserved for whatever they did that I never even saw.

I want to believe that when my son moves home, I can be the father I would have been if I hadn't been out working to keep it all together. But who am I kidding?

He will be old enough to receive mail, but too immature to toss it in the wastebasket when he doesn't want it. He'll be tall enough to reach the milk on the top shelf of the refrigerator, but too short to put it back.

The child in him will eat and walk away from the table. The adult in him will come in after 3 in the morning. The child in him will leave wet towels on the bed. The adult will say he has to grab a flight to California to "catch the rays."

No wonder we're confused over our roles. When adults wash their socks, drop off their cleaning, lend them shampoo and money, they figure it gives them rights. It gives them the right to tell them how to lead their life and pick their friends, how to dress, and what kind of a car to buy.

Rules. There will have to be rules. And once again I'll be cast into the role of the conservative, dime-squeezing, lackluster who wouldn't know how to have a good time if it was under warranty.

Good grief! Where is that woman going with my chair, and tell me how is it possible that she cannot open up her own car door but can balance a chair on her head three times her own body weight!

THE DREAM

I sunk into the sofa cushions in the living room no one ever sat in.

Part of my childhood dream was here among the books that were dusted, but never read . . . rugs that were vacuumed, but never walked on . . . flower arrangements that never died and never lived . . . draperies that were pulled to insure privacy for no one.

It's funny, but living rooms never seemed to change much. It was from such a room that my mother hid behind a curtain dividing the living room from the dining room to avoid meeting a bill collector. When I answered the door and told him my mother was not home, he looked over my shoulder, his eyes traveling the full length of the curtains, and said, "The next time your mother leaves home, tell her to take her feet with her."

It was from such a room that my father was viewed before he was buried. A long-lost cousin came to the house that day to view the remains and, looking very confused, walked up to my mother and said, "Which one is he?" Mother fought for composure and said dryly, "He's the one lying down!" Undaunted, my cousin several times removed said, "I didn't know him and I barely know you, but by God, we're family!"

The other part of that dream had just spent the weekend here . . . returning from their private worlds to reclaim their places in the most awesome, fragile, indestructible unit of feelings ever brought together under one roof: the family.

For years, anthropologists have been trying to figure out what is so compelling about the genes and drops of blood that bind a family together in a lifetime of commitment.

The relative who has no pride whatsoever in borrowing your last buck, but who runs to put in his teeth when he sees you pull into the driveway.

The grandmother who plays with the truth like a piece of bubble gum with everyone else . . . stretching it into shapes that have never been seen before . . . but who will look at your new baby and snort, "Funny-looking little thing, but maybe he'll outgrow it."

The widowed aunt who says to her husband's brother, "He loved you so and always wanted you to have his fishing gear. Just before he died he said, 'Make sure Ben gets them because he is the only one who will appreciate them.' My price to you is $300.''

The child with whom you labored sixteen hours before he decided to enter the world, who buys a $50 cashmere sweater for an airhead he has known two weeks and who gives you a meat thermometer for Mother's Day.

What is the force that keeps them returning? Is it because even if they reject, ignore, or neglect their family, they're still loved? Even when they give nothing of themselves, they're still welcome? If they've lied, been insensitive, or screwed up, they're still forgiven? Is it because their place in the family is always there for them and no one else has a right to it?

I sat there wondering what kind of a book our family would write in the year 2038. Would they remember a mother who took knots out of shoestrings with her teeth that they had wet on all day long? Or would they only remember the day she acted like a crazy lady out of control when they ate a hole in the gelatin mold she was saving for her Amway party?

Would they remember two parents who laughed, made mistakes, enjoyed sex, and didn't know the questions, let alone the answers? Or would they remember two rigid, humorless people who dedicated their lives to saying no, waxing the kitchen floor, fertilizing the lawn, and urging them to cut their hair, get a job, and stop talking with food in their mouths?

Would the sons emulate the father who stored house keys in a tackle box with a tag marking each one? Would the daughter always serve apple sauce with pork chops like it was some law handed down from her mother?

Raising a family wasn't something I put on my résumé, but I have to ask myself, would I apply for the same job again?

It was hard work. It was a lot of crud detail. It was steady. Lord, it was steady. But in retrospect, no matter what deeds my life yielded . . . no matter how many books I had written marched in a row on a library shelf, no matter how many printed words of mine dangled under magnets on refrigerator doors, I had done something rather extraordinary with my life as a mother. For three decades, I had been a matriarch of my own family . . . bonding them together, waiting for stragglers to grow up, catch up, or make up, mending verbal fences, adding a little glue for cohesion here, patching a few harsh exchanges there, and daily dispensing a potion of love and loyalty to something bigger than all of us.

My husband found me sitting in the living room and asked, ''What are you doing sitting here alone in the dark?''

''Thinking about this weekend.''

''They're good kids,'' he said reassuringly as he sat beside me. I rested my head on his shoulder.

He added softly, "The snake is gone. It escaped from the cage in the utility room."

I didn't move. Then I whispered without emotion, "We are selling the house, and those sick, ungrateful kids will never see us again."

Drawing my knees up under my chin, I assumed a fetal position. I would remain in this position until the snake was found no matter how long it took.

Why did we continually test one another's patience, loyalty, and love? Could it be that's what the survival of a family is based upon?

The room was getting chilly. A car went by and its lights illuminated the room, then threw it again into darkness. I thought about the kids again and hoped with all my heart that they would someday aspire, as I did, to the dream of a family of their own and a living room that no one ever sat in.

Fulfillment? Immortality? Revenge?

What do you think?

About the Author

Erma Bombeck's column, "At Wit's End," was one of the most widely syndicated in the world. Her books have sold nearly three million copies in hardcover and *many* millions of copies in paperback. Ms. Bombeck died on April 22, 1996.

IF LIFE IS A BOWL OF CHERRIES— WHAT AM I DOING IN THE PITS?

I will never understand children. I never pretended to. I meet mothers all the time who make resolutions to themselves. "I'm going to develop patience with my children and go out of my way to show them I am interested in them and what they do. I am going to understand my children." These women wind up making rag rugs, using blunt scissors.

I have never understood, for example, how come a child can climb up on the roof, scale the TV antenna and rescue the cat . . . yet cannot walk down the hallway without grabbing both walls with his grubby hands for balance.

Or how come a child can eat yellow snow, kiss the dog on the lips, chew gum that he found in the ashtray, but refuse to drink from a glass his brother has just used.

Why is it he can stand with one foot on first base while reaching out and plucking a baseball off the ground with the tips of his fingers . . . yet he cannot pick up a piece of soap before it melts into the drain.

I've seen kids ride bicycles, run, play ball, set up a camp, swing, fight a war, swim, and race for eight hours . . . yet have to be driven to the garbage can.

It puzzles me how a child can see a dairy bar three miles away, but cannot see a 4 x 6 rug that has scrunched up under his feet and has been dragged through two rooms. Maybe you know why a child can reject a hot dog with mustard served on a soft bun at home, yet eat six of them two hours later at fifty cents each.

I firmly believe kids don't want your understanding. They want your trust, your compassion, your blinding love and your car keys, but try to understand them and you're in big trouble.

THE GRASS IS ALWAYS GREENER OVER THE SEPTIC TANK

...The suburban lawn not only became an obsession with the suburban husband, it became the very symbol of manhood. Not to have a lawn was like admitting you turned off the Super Bowl to take a nap, used deodorant shields in your T-shirts, or had training wheels on your Harley-Davidson. Every casual greeting opened with: "How's the lawn, Buddy?" "Hey, Frank, see you got your crabgrass on the run." Or "Set your blade down an inch, Buck. We all did."

...One evening as Lyle was tooling around in his riding mower with the reclining bucket seats and the console dashboard—his automatic sprinkler creeping along silently over the green carpet, his hedges topped perfectly with his electric hedge clipper, his trees being fed automatically just the right amounts of iron and nitrogen—his neighbor dropped by and said, "Too bad about your lawn, Lyle."

Lyle shut off his motor and paled slightly. "What do you mean, 'Too bad about my lawn'?"

"The whole neighborhood is talking about it. I thought you knew."

"Knew what? For God's sake tell me."

"Your lawn has root rot nematode."

Lyle's eyes misted. "Are you sure?"

"Didn't you see the little brown spots that never seemed to get better when you watered them?"

"And it's such a young lawn," said Lyle. "How long does it have?"

"With no bicycles, sleds, or kids running over it, I give it about a year."

"Well, we're not going to give up," said Lyle, squaring his shoulders, "they come up with new things every day. We're going to fight!" he said, heading out toward the garden center.

"Hey," yelled his neighbor, "maybe this isn't the time to bring it up, but I heard your ex-wife is getting remarried."

Lyle turned slowly, disgust written plainly on his face. "What kind of animal are you?" he asked, his voice quavering with emotion. "First you come here and tell me my lawn has root rot nematode and there's nothing anyone can do to save it and at best it only has a year to live, and then you babble on about my wife remarrying. Who cares? Don't you understand? If my lawn dies, I don't want to go on living any more. Leave me alone."

As his neighbor retreated, Lyle got down on his hands and knees and sobbed, "We'll travel. That's what we'll do—just you and me. We'll visit the White House lawn, the grounds at Mt. Vernon, maybe upper New York State where the grass is green most of the time and you can make new friends..."

I LOST EVERYTHING IN THE POST-NATAL DEPRESSION

I try, but somehow I am always the woman in the wrong line.

I am always behind the shopper at the grocery store who has stitched her coupons in the lining of her coat and wants to talk about a "strong" chicken she bought two weeks ago. The register tape also runs out just before her sub-total.

In the public rest-room, I always stand behind the teen-ager who is changing into her band uniform for a parade and doesn't emerge until she has combed the tassels on her boots, shaved her legs, and recovered her contact lens from the commode.

In the confessional, there is only one person ahead of me. A priest. Now who could be safer following a priest into the confessional? Anyone but me. My priest has just witnessed a murder, has not made his Easter duty since 1967, and wants to talk about his mixed marriage.

At my bank the other day I cruised up and down a full five minutes trying to assess the customers. There was the harried secretary with a handful of deposit slips. I'd be a fool to get behind her. At the other window was a small businessman with a canvas bag of change. I figured he had probably drained a wishing well somewhere and brought three years of pennies in to be wrapped. In the next line was an elderly gent who seemed familiar with everyone. He was obviously going to visit his money and his safety deposit box.

I slipped in behind a little tyke with no socks, dirty gym shoes, and a Smile sweatshirt. He had to be a thirty-second transaction.

The kid had not made a deposit since the first grade. He had lost his passbook. His records were not in the bank's regular accounts but were in the school section. He did not know his passbook number or his homeroom teacher's name, as she had been married near the beginning of the school year. Each of 2,017 cards of the school's enrollment had to be flipped. He deposited twenty-five cents.

He hesitated as he looked at his book, noting he had made fifteen cents in interest. He wished to withdraw it. As he was only old enough to print, he needed his mother's permission. His mother was called on the phone, which took some time, as she was drinking coffee at a neighbor's home. She said no.

He then wanted to know if he could see where they kept his money and if he could have one of the free rain bonnets they advertised. He asked directions to a drinking fountain and left— twenty minutes later.

AT WIT'S END

"I say, you didn't cut your bangs at home with pinking shears or anything, did you?" she asked suspiciously.

"Oh no," I said. "I just want my hair done because I've been a little depressed since the baby was born."

"Oh," she said softly, "how old is your baby?"

"Twenty-four," I answered.

Because I was unknown to the shop, I drew Miss Lelanie, who had been out of beauty school three days—this time. (The lawsuit with the nasty bald woman is still pending.) With Miss Lelanie, I felt as relaxed as a cat in a roomful of rocking chairs. She flipped through my hair like she was tossing a wilted salad. Finally she called in Mr. Miriam to show him what she had found. Both concurred that my ends were split, my scalp diseased, and I was too far over the hill to manufacture a decent supply of hair oil.

"It's all that dry?" I asked incredulously.

"I'd stay away from careless smokers," said Miss Lelanie without smiling.

Miss Lelanie massaged, combed, conditioned, rolled, brushed, teased, and sprayed for the better part of two hours. Then she whirled me around to look into the mirror. "Why fight it?" I said, pinching the reflection's cheek. "You're a sex symbol." Miss Lelanie closed her eyes as if asking for divine guidance.

I don't mind admitting I felt like a new woman as I walked across the plush carpet, my shoulders squared, my head held high. I could feel every pair of eyes in the room following me.

"Pardon me, honey," said Miss Lelanie, "you're dragging a piece of the bathroom tissue on your heel. Want me to throw it away?"

"JUST WAIT TILL YOU HAVE CHILDREN OF YOUR OWN"
with Bil Keane

"If you don't go to sleep," my own mother used to threaten, "the tooth fairy Mafia will pull all your teeth and sell them in the black market." Or, "You wet the bed one more time and a rainbow will follow you around for the rest of your life."

The other day I called Mother in desperation. "I need help," I said. "I've used every threat on my kids you ever used on me and I've run out. Do you have anything stronger that you held out on me?"

AUNT ERMA'S COPE BOOK

Ever since I read that Eva Braun (Hitler's mistress), Judas Iscariot, and Anne Boleyn shared my zodiac sign, I could never get too choked up about Astrology.

Mr. Steve meant well, but he didn't know what a loser I was. My sun never rose on my sign. My planets were always conspiring behind my back. And my destiny always read like it had been out in the natal sun too long.

Maybe I was just bitter, but it always seemed like other people got the good signs. Their horoscopes always read "Popularity and untold wealth will haunt you. There is no getting away from it. You are irresistible to every sign in the zodiac. Give in and enjoy."

Not mine. It was always an ominous warning like "Watch your purse." "Your high school acne was only in remission, and will return the fifteenth of the month." "Don't become discouraged by your friends who will take advantage of you."

Somehow, I always felt if Mother had held on a little longer—a good month and a half—things would have been different for me...